PRAISE FOR DREAM BIG

"Casey Gwinn's work with women and families that are survivors of domestic abuse is nothing short of extraordinary. I have been inspired by his vision and dedication to ending the cycle of violence against women in this country and I hope *Dream Big* will inspire others as well."

—*Reese Witherspoon, Actress, Avon Global Ambassador*

"Casey Gwinn and Gael Strack are leading the way forward in the domestic violence movement. They are challenging us to think outside the box; to keep growing, changing, and evolving as we work to prevent family violence. *Dream Big* is their most powerful book yet. It sets a high standard for every community in continuing to listen to survivors and then respond with the services they need delivered in the most accessible way possible."

—*Sarah Buel, Survivor, Advocate, Law Professor*

"Every police chief and law enforcement policy maker in America should read *Dream Big*. Casey Gwinn and Gael Strack remind us so forcefully that domestic violence is a public safety issue and we will not stop it until every law enforcement agency starts working much more closely with district attorneys, judges, shelter advocates, business leaders, and other service providers. *Dream Big* challenges us all to be in the life saving business together."

—*Lt. Mark Wynn (Ret.), Nashville Metro Police Department*

DREAM BIG

A Simple, Complicated Idea to Stop Family Violence

CASEY GWINN

with GAEL STRACK

Dream Big: A Simple, Complicated Idea to Stop Family Violence

Published by Wheatmark®
610 East Delano Street, Suite 104, Tucson, Arizona 85705 U.S.A.
www.wheatmark.com

ISBN: 978-1-60494-452-5
LCCN: 2010924827

rev201001

Dedication

Mabel married Gardner soon after his first wife died during child-birth. She had never been married, but she was taken with this young widower with two small children. He was a businessman with dreams and aspirations—and a broken heart after the death of his first wife. He courted Mabel; they fell in love and soon married. Mabel wanted to care for Gardner and his sons, but she also wanted her own children. Within two years, she was pregnant. Over the course of the next 12 years, she gave birth to six children of her own.

Gardner was not abusive with Mabel at first. He was a firm discipli-narian with the children, but he did not raise a hand toward her until later in their marriage. His anger and rage were potent. No child ever wanted to cross him. The consequences were swift and unequivocal. Later, the adult children recalled his tongue lashings, name calling, and physical abuse. One child much later recalled ushering her younger brother out of the room when mom and dad began to argue. The youngest child remem-bered dad throwing things at his mother. One daughter remembered the radio being turned up so the children could not hear the arguments. And each of them remembered, like it was yesterday, their father saying over and over, "Quit your crying or I'll give you something to cry about." The youngest child mastered the strategy and used it later in life, like many other parents in his generation, on his own children.

The children grew up not knowing that healthy families did not function like the family ruled by Gardner. They grew up thinking their family was like all others. They lived through the many experiences of a home with varying levels of emotional, verbal, and physical abuse, even as America came to grips with the ugly secrets of a patriarchal, male-dominated society where abusive conduct was used systematically to control both women and children. Sorting it out was never simple. Gardner was not a monster. He was not always abusive. He taught his children the value of hard work. The youngest boy would later tell his son of being kicked down the hallway by his father so hard one time that every kick lifted him off the ground. Yet, that same boy would also teach his son the value of hard work…that he learned from his often abusive father. His father's firmness was balanced by love and care from his mother. Gardner had a strong faith and deeply held beliefs about family, commitment, and perseverance that later took his children far in life.

The details of Gardner's abusive ways have never been fully documented. Mabel took her eyewitness accounts to the grave and never disclosed what she endured. The children did not even begin to discuss the potential impacts until the suspected suicide of one of the brothers. As one of the older sons spent his last days in hospice care (at age 81), he disclosed for the first time to his youngest brother their father's verbal and emotional abuse that he had carried with him his whole life. His mother had died giving birth to him. Throughout his entire life, his father blamed him for his mother's death. It was a deep, deep wound. As the two boys talked in hospice, they debated whether their father would be in heaven. The youngest boy later acknowledged actions of his father that today would be prosecuted. But even he hesitated to call it violence or hitting. It was a painful admission that he needed to minimize and rationalize, even as the "junk in the attic" that each child carried into adulthood, out of Gardner and Mabel's home, slowly came out over the years.

And as noted, the baggage was not all bad. There was faith in Gardner and Mabel's home. Gardner taught the boys the value of perseverance and determination. He taught them to play tennis, to garden, to be handy around the house, and to make a goal and pursue it. He was a successful businessman and church leader. Mabel was a towering woman of prayer and faith who passed on to her children a strong commitment to serving the needy and putting faith into action in the face of great difficulty. Surely such good things should not be ignored or the family shamed by disclosing the ugly underside of verbally, emotionally, and physically abusive conduct in the home. But the story of Gardner and Mabel is an important story—first, because they raised those children and sent them off to raise children of their own during the budding feminist movement of the 1940s, 1950s, and 1960s. Second, they are important because they remind us how gray family violence can be. It is not always black and white. The bad guys are many times also good guys. The families with ugly secrets and unhealthy, dysfunctional behavior often have many positive, redeeming attributes. Finally, Gardner and Mabel are important because they are my grandparents. The youngest boy in that home was my dad.

This book is dedicated to Rev. William D. Gwinn. He died April 17, 2009 at Desert Regional Medical Center in Palm Springs after a massive heart attack. But before he died, he loved my Mom for 58 years of marriage and he began to break the cycle that my grandfather perpetuated. He built a camp for high school students that is still a national model. He loved people and he loved his God. He wasn't perfect. He made some mistakes and struggled with some demons from his childhood, but he was my hero.

When Dad died last spring, I felt lost. I felt like my anchor, my foundation, my moral compass was gone. My dad gave me my manhood. He instilled in me his values. He passed on to me the teachings of Jesus. When I was young, he was my protector. As I grew older, he was my encourager, my affirmer, and the supporter of my dreams. In fact, he taught me how to dream big. He modeled for me how to see things as they could be, not as they are. He modeled for me, both good and bad, what a father is, what a husband is, and what a man acts like. And when he died, all the bad stuff didn't matter anymore. The ways I reduced contact in later years to protect myself emotionally faded away. The resentment I had for the emotionally abusive things he sometimes said evaporated. The frustration I sometimes felt when our visits did not go well…it was all gone. Only my last kiss on his forehead stuck in my mind, the last time I told him I loved him, the promise I made to him the night before he died that I would take care of everything and that he didn't need to worry about my mom or the house or the bills or the future. I would become the man now. I would be the protector and provider. I would be the encourager and affirmer and supporter of dreams.

So, Dad, I love you. I hope this book and my life will make you proud. You began the journey to break the cycle of verbal, emotional, and physical abuse that you were born into. By the grace of God, I, my children, and my grandchildren, will finish what you started.

CASEY GWINN
JULY 2010

Contents

Acknowledgements

It is always an impossible task to thank everyone who has played a role in making a book possible. Hundreds of dedicated friends, supporters, colleagues, survivors, and other professionals have played a role in helping us do the work that now fills the pages of this book. Special thanks to Beth Gwinn, Jan Strack, Mehry Mohseni, and Melissa Mack for their editing, input, and support. Grael Norton and Kat Gautreaux at Wheatmark deserve high marks for helping to get this book into print in just weeks after we submitted it for consideration. We are also deeply indebted to the small but mighty team at the National Family Justice Center Alliance including Robert Keetch, Jennifer Anderson, Brenda Lugo, Melissa Mack, Mehry Mohseni, Lori Gillam, Alexia Peters, Michelle Adams, and Yvonne Coiner. The planners who have helped us start so many Family Justice Centers around the world deserve to be recognized including Judi Adams, Glen Price, Phil Eastman, and so many others that we don't have room to name. The richness of our thinking about co-located services for victims of domestic violence and their children has been helped immeasurably by our team of national advisors—Dr. Oliver Williams, Denise Gamache, Dr. Dean Hawley, Mike Mason, Kim Wells, Yvonne Carrasco, Nancy O'Malley, Sarah Buel, and Sue Else. Sue Else, the President of the National Network to End Domestic Violence, has provided much insight, critical feedback, and thoughtful advice that has shaped many of the concepts in our vision and work. We must also recognize Robert Martin, Ashley Walker, and Mike Scogin—three of our long-time members of the Operating Board of the Alliance who have helped us figure out how to develop as an organization and a social change force.

Many will never meet them but our VOICES Committee of survivors at the San Diego Family Justice Center are truly the unsung heroes of this work and this book—always challenging us, always willing to share their stories, always willing to help us evaluate what works and what does not work in helping women, men, and children who have faced violence and abuse. As we will discuss in the book, the San Diego Family Justice Center had a few years of struggle and re-invention after the first five years of operation. We must acknowledge Police Chief Bill Lansdowne, Capt. Guy Swanger, Lt. Lori Luhnow and Sgt. Judy Woods from the San Diego Police Department for their commitment to rebuild the service delivery model after it faltered for a time because of poor leadership. We must also recognize the Mayor of San Diego and City Council for their support for the vision as well as those who have played critical roles in the history of the Center—some who are still involved and others who have moved on—Charles Wilson, Verna Griffin Tabor, Bonnie Pearson, Jim Barker, Diane Mc-Grogan, Kimberly Pearce, Kimberly Weisz, Dr. Diane Lass, Kristine Rowe, Mickey Stonier, Tom Collins, Katie Zumwalt, Jackie Dietz, Amy Fitzpatrick, Janet Bowermaster, John Landsverk, Carolyn Wilson, and many others. The hundreds of volunteers and supporters who raised money for the San Diego Family Justice Center as the innovative idea evolved will always be remembered.

Thanks to so many original local funders and now national funders who have helped us launch, refine, and define the vision and the work of co-located services including the California Endowment, Alliance Healthcare, Verizon Wireless, the Waitt Family Foundation, EDCO Disposal, Qualcomm, National University, Cox Communications, Jerome's Furniture, the Verizon Foundation, the Avon Foundation,

Blueshield of California Foundation, the U.S. Department of Justice, Vital Voices Global Partnership, and many more. Caring people in many of those organizations have played powerful roles in helping us think out our journey and the way to make our dream a reality. We want to thank Patrick Gaston, Lupita Reyes, Melody Brown, Carol Kurzig, Mary Quinn, Christine Jaworsky, Bess Bendet, Dr. Jerry Lee, Susan Williams, Shireen Zaman, and others who have helped advocate for funding for pieces of our dream.

We must also acknowledge as we will later in the book some of the powerful people who have helped shape our lives—many of whom have played key roles in the battered women's movement in this country over the last forty years. They include women like Susan Schecter, Del Martin, Lenore Walker, Ruth Gottstein, Ellen Pence, Esta Soler, Barbara Hart, Rita Smith, Sheryl Cates, Lynn Rosenthal, Joan Zorza, Catherine Pierce, Cindy Dyer, Susan Kelly-Dreiss, Ann Menard, Jacquelyn Campbell, Felicia Collins-Correia, Ashley Walker, Mary Lauby, Tiffany Carr, Colleen Coble, Debby Tucker, and others who have trained us, challenged us, or shared their books, articles, or critiques with us.

We should also recognize the important men in the domestic violence movement who have also helped us move forward. Special thanks goes to Dr. Oliver Williams, Dr. Jeff Edleson, Jackson Katz, Ben Atherton-Zeman, Ted Bunch, Jim Henderson, Mark Wynn, John Welter, Ulester Douglas, Judge Ron Adrine, and many others. And of course, special thanks goes to Rebecca Lovelace, Susan Adams, Nadia Lockyer, Lt. Chris Sayers, Judy Bell, Kate Reeves, Asha Parekh, Joanne Fine, Meera Ballal, Pam Weaner, Jo Ricchiuti, Hannah Sassoon, Nikki Daniels, Linda Ray, Amy Dilworth, and Mary Claire Landry. These folks are among the pioneers of Family Justice Centers and other co-located service models who have worked with us to see how the ideas apply in their communities.

This book is because of all of you who believed that together we could be more effective than separately, who believed that victims should be listened to when they said they wanted their services in one place, and who believed that we could overcome differences, dis-

xiv   Acknowledgements

agreements, and conflicts in order to make the dream of coordinated community response and co-located services a reality in local communities. And to the thousands of survivors who continue to share their stories and provide direction and guidance in all we do...thank you for holding us accountable for meeting your needs.

Introduction

Sarah Buel was on welfare, living with an abusive man, caring for a small baby, and determined that someday her life would be different. She deserved better. She deserved the best. She was beaten down by her abuser, by circumstances, by her family history, and by the indifference of many around her. But she was a dreamer. She kept the candle of hope burning in her heart even through the darkest times. She drove by Harvard University and yelled from inside the car, "You are going to let me in." And they did. She determined to go to Harvard Law School when relatives said women could be legal secretaries but not lawyers. At Harvard, she created one of the first student-led Domestic Violence Legal Clinics in America. She became a prosecutor in Quincy, Massachusetts and created one of the first model prosecution programs in the nation for dealing with misdemeanor and felony domestic violence cases. She stood up in the face of injustice and she rallied public officials to stand with her. She refused to take "No" for an answer. She rejected, "This is the way we do things", and "We cannot afford that." She went on to travel the country and world sharing her story and challenging people to dream bigger and expect more from their systems. Some people laughed at her. Once during a speech I sat in of Sarah's, when she started talking about seeing money streaming toward her and quoted from Essence Magazine, the woman next to me laughed out loud at Sarah's audacity and seeming relentless optimism. But Sarah didn't let the naysayers or the critics or the negative energy of little people stop her. She kept clamoring for change. And she has not stopped. Recently, she served as a law professor at the University of Texas School of Law. While there, she started another student-staffed legal clinic for victims of abuse. She continues to challenge everyone she meets to dream bigger, do more, and expect more. In every community, she challenges agencies to come together, work together, and figure out how to collaborate more effectively in order to help victims of domestic violence and their children. Today, she is serving as the Director of the Diane Halle Center for Family Justice at the Sandra Day O'Connor College of Law at Arizona State University. Sarah Buel knows how to dream big and she should be an example to every person reading this book. She is one of the many who have touched my life in the last 25 years of working to stop family violence. And she embodies the spirit of what this book is all about. Learn from others, listen to survivors, dream big, and change the world. God Bless, Sarah Buel. She is one of the many voices of survivors who have laid the foundation for the ever growing development and improvement of co-located services for victims of abuse and their children in America and around the world."

We need to stop domestic violence. The dream in this book is one key way to stop violence in intimate relationships. It is about bringing everyone together in a community. It is about locating all the services that victims and their children need in one place instead of making them go from agency to agency and place to place, telling their story over and over. It is about something called a Family Justice Center but such places can have many different names and each one can and should be unique to each individual community that pursues the big dream. If you are new to the Family Justice Center world, welcome! If you work in or currently support a Center or a similar type of domestic violence agency or shelter that brings together many services in one place, welcome! This book is an easy read. In three to four hours, you can "get it" about why bringing services to one place is the best way to help victims of abuse and trauma. You can learn some of the lessons we have learned from working in communities across the

United States and around the world. Hopefully, we will help you stay motivated if you are already connected to a collaborative community approach to family violence. If you are not yet part of planning a new Center or supporting an existing Center or agency doing similar kinds of multi-disciplinary work to stop family violence, we hope you will get motivated to be part of this journey with us.

In this book we will often use the term Family Justice Center but we use it very generically. We use it to talk about all kinds of models of co-location and multi-agency partnerships where individuals and agencies come together in one place to make it easier for victims and their children to get help. The principles can apply with child abuse, sexual assault, elder abuse, human trafficking, and other kinds of abuse as well though our primary focus is family violence.

The Family Justice Center is a very simple idea…that is very complicated…and very hard to turn into a reality—all the services that a victim of domestic violence might need under one roof. Some call it "services under one roof", while others refer to it as a "shopping mall" for victims and their children. Some call it a "one stop shop" though we don't like that term. Services in the arena of family violence often make the difference between life and death. They are complex and must be uniquely tailored to meet the needs of each client. "One stop shop" seems to demean the importance of the work to us. But whether they are referred to as "one place" or "under one roof" or "co-located, multi-agency" services, the approach can include as many appropriate services as a victim needs in one place. Civil attorneys, advocates, counselors, police officers, prosecutors, chaplains, nurses, doctors, employment training professionals, community volunteers, and other kinds of service providers can all be available to help a victim together. Domestic violence shelters and community-based agencies started down the road of having services in one place many years ago but no one had brought together staff from twenty-seven agencies until we did it in San Diego in 2002. San Diego did not invent the concept of co-located services. San Diego just took it to a different level with staff from twenty seven agencies all working together in one place. One of the matriarchs of the battered women's movement, Ellen Pence, has dedicated much of her career to helping communities coordinate all their services in models called "CCR" or coordinated community response. Ellen Pence has called Family Justice Centers "coordinated community response on steroids." It is a fitting description.

Within five years of opening the most comprehensive co-located services model in the history of the domestic violence movement in 2002, the San Diego Family Justice Center was serving 1,200 families per month. Survivors in San Diego were praising the model in focus groups and exit interviews. They felt safer, more supported, and more empowered to manage their own lives. Domestic violence homicides were declining. Conviction rates of offenders were rising. And agencies were working more effectively together than they ever had before.

Soon after the opening of the San Diego Family Justice Center, Oprah Winfrey profiled the Center on her syndicated television show. Within months, the co-located services concept was traveling around the world. Only months after that, President George W. Bush created a national initiative in the United States to create fifteen more Centers based on the San Diego model but uniquely tailored to their own communities. In 2005, Congress added Family Justice Centers to the Violence Against Women Act and authorized the U.S. Department of Justice to provide funding to Centers and similar kinds of multi-agency service models. Since then, many other communities that were not selected in the President's Initiative have pursued the idea on their own based on the model in San Diego. Existing domestic violence programs too heard the call and started reaching out to more partner agencies and identifying other service providers they could have at the existing facilities. Some shelters and local agencies had already been co-locating services with other agencies but now they began to accelerate their efforts. A movement was launched and began to gain ground quickly.

In 2006, we published the first book on the rapidly developing Family Justice Center movement, *"Hope for Hurting Families: Creating Family Justice Centers Across America."* (available at www.familyjusticecenter.org). At the time we had nearly fifteen Centers open around the United States, modeled after the San Diego Family Justice Center. The first book was an in-depth look at the entire philosophical backdrop for Family Justice Centers. It was a hard read for many who did not work in the field of domestic violence but it was our effort to fully enunciate the need for such Centers, the philosophy behind the Centers, and the critical elements for having a successful Center. Most of the book was focused on the lessons learned from opening the San Diego Family Justice Center.

Today, we have over sixty Centers open and operating in the United States and other Centers in the United Kingdom, Canada, Mexico, and Jordan. Beyond these operational Centers, there are over one hundred communities in the United States and more than ten other countries that are planning Family Justice Centers or similar types of Centers. Some communities have one such Center, larger communities have multiple Centers. Some Centers are coordinated by community-based domestic violence shelters. Other Centers are coordinated by Police Departments or District Attorney's Offices. Depending on whom the lead agency is in a community, and the unique characteristics of a community, every Center looks different and has different services and different partner agencies. The core design is driven by asking survivors in a community if they want their services in one location and then asking them what services they would like to have available in one place. It is a very simple idea…that is very difficult to actually implement in a community. But when it is done right, it is a powerful, effective, and comprehensive approach to helping victims and their children. It also makes it much easier to hold abusers accountable for their violence when everyone is working closely together.

So, this book, our fourth book in the last four years, is an effort to explain the "why" of Family Justice Centers in a very simple, short concise volume that can be read in a few hours. It borrows some from the first book and adds more from the successes of the many Family Justice Centers and similar models of service delivery now operating in the United States and around the world. But the focus of the new book remains on the "Why?" Why are Family Justice Centers and other types of multi-agency service delivery models effective? Why are they needed? Why do victims want to receive their services in one place? What feedback are they providing about how effective such Centers can be in helping meet their needs? Why should a community invest the time and energy in this model? Why is it less expensive to provide services in a multi-agency, co-located service delivery approach? What are the guiding principles behind such Centers and why do those principles matter when you start operating a Center? What have we learned so far in this movement toward more co-located services and why should the lessons learned help shape the future of developing and operating Family Justice Centers?

We have also published two "how" manuals in the last three years—one in English, one in Arabic (available at www.familyjustice-center.org). These manuals focus on how to create a Family Justice Center. How do you bring everyone together to plan it? How do you design it? How do you fund it? How do you promote it? How do you operate it? How do you sustain it? How do you keep a Center healthy? How do you keep a Center or multi-agency collaborative service model focused on the needs of its clients? How do you ensure the guiding principles are implemented every day in the operation of a Center? How do you protect the work and vision and ensure that it does not collapse when a leader changes or local elected officials turn over? How does the concept work in the West, versus Europe, Central America, South America, Asia, or the Middle East?

Though I (Casey) am the primary author of the "Why?" books and Gael Strack is the primary author of the "How?" books, we work hard to list both of us on every book because we have been honored and humbled to be part of this movement now for over a decade and to work together in the field of family violence prevention for nearly 25 years. Much of this book is written in the first person when I am writing. When Gael has written a chapter, we acknowledge it at the beginning, but all of it is the result of...coming together...and sticking together...for all these years. I have often been the "Dream Big" guy and Gael has often been the "Start Small" gal. Sometimes my ideas are impractical and too unmanageable. Gael has always been the one to figure that out and then figure out what can be done and how it should work. We have spent much time over the years dreaming together, thinking together, learning from our mistakes together, and, yes, laughing together as much as possible. We have had to deal with strains, tensions, and challenges in our relationship—just like folks working together in Family Justice Centers. We have offended each other, and had to seek forgiveness—just like folks working in Family Justice Centers. We have taken each other for granted and had to work through it and reconcile—just like folks in Family Justice Centers. We have had to stay humble and work hard to listen to each other and find common ground even when we both thought we were right—like folks in Family Justice Centers. We have, however, persevered. With the support of our loving spouses, and the dedication of many friends in this movement, we have kept learning, kept growing, kept listening to survivors, kept asking how we can do better, and kept moving forward.

Gael and I have also had the opportunity to work with many amazing people, in San Diego, across the United States, and around the world. We mention many of them in the Acknowledgements and many others are quoted throughout this book—professionals, survivors, philanthropists, elected officials, policy makers, caring corporations, and local community activists that have committed themselves to the vision and the hard work of figuring out how to provide more services in less places for those in need.

As you read this book, you will also find that we have included many stories of survivors. The stories come from those who have received services in Family Justice Centers and other types of multi-agency models. Stories provide context, evidence, and direction for this movement based on the lived experience of real people caught in the cross-fire of family violence. Our first FJC researcher, Dr. John Landsverk, said to us early on, "When you have a few stories, you have anecdotes, but when you have 5,000 stories you have research data. And research data will shape and direct the entire Family Justice Center movement." He was right on the money. We have taken his comments to heart. So, you will see stories and quotes from real clients in real places receiving day to day services in co-located service models.

The honest, direct feedback from survivors and their children drives the Family Justice Center movement. Today, we conservatively estimate that the existing Centers in the United States and other countries have served over 150,000 victims of domestic violence and their children—women, children, and men have received services at Family Justice Centers. And many of the stories have been captured and the feedback has been documented. Victims of domestic violence and their children want their services coordinated and they want them co-located if at all possible in a community. Because of the consistent positive feedback of victims and the support of professionals who are experiencing the benefits, the Family Justice Center concept is here to stay—a progressive, thoughtful way to bring together all the services that a victim needs in one place.

These are exciting times in the United States and around the world. Awareness of issues about violence against men, women, and children is probably at an all time high. As we write this, the Obama Administration is seeking to significantly increase federal spending on issues surrounding domestic violence in the United States. The President has named Lynn Rosenthal as the first White House advisor in history on Violence Against Women Issues. Vice-President Joe Biden brings a louder voice to the White House and the federal government than there has ever been at such a high level of government. The Office on Violence Against Women (OVW) in the U.S Department of Justice is spending more time on big picture thinking than at perhaps any time in its history. The new Director, Judge Susan Carbon, brings new energy and vision to OVW based on her real life experience dealing with victims and abusers. Secretary of State Clinton has named Melanne Verveer, the former President of Vital Voices Global Partnership, as the Senior Coordinator for Women's Issues at the State Department. Major corporate and philanthropic funders like the Avon Foundation, Verizon, Robert Wood Johnson, the Annie E. Casey Foundation, Blue Shield of California Foundation, and others are starting to think much more strategically about their giving and how to maximize their impact and how to push the domestic violence movement forward toward greater social change.

This book is intended to be a contribution to one area in all this strategic thinking. It is focused on one aspect of this ever changing movement on the planet to deal with intimate partner violence. It is focused on our dream and the dream of many others that in the years to come victims of family violence will get more and more of their services in Family Justice Centers or other kinds of co-located service models.

We dream of a day when every community in America and many communities in countries around the world, have a place or a few places where many services are provided under one roof. We pray for a day when victims don't have to go from agency to agency to agency in their search for assistance, support, and safety. We believe that the day can come when Family Justice Centers are commonplace and serve as a living testimony that individuals, disciplines, and agencies can come together—set aside ego, turf, and personality conflicts—and change the world for victims of family violence and their children. You can be part of the dream, you can be our answer to prayer, you can believe with us. And we have little doubt that if enough people join us, if enough people commit themselves to the vision…it will become a reality and millions of hurting families will one day experience the joy of life without violence and abuse.

CASEY GWINN AND GAEL STRACK
JULY 2010

CHAPTER ONE

We Must Honor and Respect, Then We Can Help

My name is Rachel and I was a victim of domestic violence. I lived with someone who physically and emotionally abused me. I had a near-death experience, not once, but twice! But, I'm one of the lucky ones; I survived, I got away. My near-death experience brought me to a special and safe place. This place is the Family Justice Center—a place where victims of domestic violence can get their lives back together again, that provides legal and medical services for those who are in need. My recovery started with me. I had to start my life over again with the help of many caring people. Then I found out I was pregnant with my second child. I had to choose to get healthy again not only for me, but for my children. My daughter became the first Family Justice Center baby. The Family Justice Center gave me many resources so we could be safe from my abuser. My life has had many changes, but through the Family Justice Center and the great people that work there I can stand on my own two feet again. I'm a proud mother and have learned how not to be a victim. Through the last two years, I have done many great things. I have given back to our community; spoken at a national domestic violence conference; and been featured in Nurse Zone.com. I am now humbly grateful for the many positive changes and I can now live a happy and healthy life without being a victim. Thanks to the Family Justice Center concept...Freedom!

This book is about why we need Family Justice Centers and other types of co-located service models in America and around the world to help stop family violence. It explains what they are and why they are a critical part of the future. The title tells it all. We need to DREAM BIG in the journey to stopping violence in our families. But the second half of the title is also important. It is a SIMPLE... COMPLICATED idea to bring all the services to one place in a community. It is simple because...it is simple. Everybody should be in one place. If you ask victims of domestic violence in any community in America or around the world if they would like to go one place for all the help they need or go many places—they ALWAYS say one place! So, advocating for such a simple idea seems...SIMPLE. But it is complicated because bringing all the agencies together is really hard work. Different organizational values, different work cultures, different focus areas, different belief systems, different ways of approaching the work, different legal obligations...from each partner agency you would want to bring into a co-located Center... makes the Family Justice Center concept very...COMPLICATED.

This book seeks to lay it out from start to finish for everyone who cares about stopping family violence, because the simple, complicated Family Justice Center idea is working in communities across the United States and around the world. How do we know that? Survivors are telling us it is working! And we now have good outcome studies starting to document what co-located services mean in the lives of victims and their kids.[1] It should not be a surprise. A new study has already documented how much domestic violence shelters, particularly those with multi-disciplinary services, means for victims and their children.[2] Wrapping a victim in services works.

But before we dive into the growing, expanding vision for co-located services, we need to talk a little bit about what domestic violence is and what we need to know about our own beliefs as a culture before we race off to advocate for the co-located, multi-agency service idea or other types of collaborations in order to help victims and their children. In the next two chapters we must address three topics before we talk about the journey to co-located services and Family Justice Centers. In this chapter, we will look at our biases against victims and look at how to honor them and treat them with respect. In the next chapter, we will look at the history of the domestic violence movement and seek to understand the foundation that has produced the powerful movement toward Family Justice Centers and other types of co-located service models.

A number of years ago, my friend Elaine Weiss published an excellent book devoted to providing practical advice and support to friends in need.[3] It is a must-read for anyone who wants to provide practical help to others victimized by family violence. The goal in this chapter is less ambitious. We need to understand our biases toward battered women before we rush forward to offer support and we need to understand how critical it is to respect and honor victims of family violence and their children before we try to help them.

ADMITTING OUR BIAS AGAINST BATTERED WOMEN

So, let me just get it out there right from the beginning of this book: *Our culture still has a profound bias against battered women.* Even after over 40 years of the women's movement and the battered women's movement, we must be honest with each other and with ourselves. Many in our society still don't like battered women. Some professional women who have never been victims say they would never let a man hit them. Some law enforcement professionals are tired of dealing with them. Some pastors, priests, and rabbis see them as spiritually weak and needy. Some medical professionals see them as expensive (and often uninsured).

Del Martin first called out many of these biases in 1977 in her seminal book, *Battered Wives*.[4] Susan Schecter talked again of these biases in 1982 when she identified sexism as a core issue in trying to address domestic violence. She called out how medical professionals liked to label victims neurotic, hysteric, hypochondriac, or mentally ill.[5] Schecter identified tendencies toward victim blaming theories and victim provocation theories.[6] And many others have written and spoken on these biases over the years. But they are not gone yet and we must continue to acknowledge them in order to understand what powerful barriers they become to helping victims and their children.

One colleague of mine has said, "The first time you are hit you are a victim; the second time you are a volunteer"[7]—a provocative but dangerous statement when actually spoken to domestic violence victims in the midst of abuse. It, like so many other views, still leads us invariably toward some form of victim blaming. Oprah Winfrey, who has done so much to help domestic violence victims over the years, called relationships with violence and abuse the "sick dance" when I appeared on her show in 2003. During the show she asked many victims she interviewed what they did to provoke or facilitate the abuse. To be fair, Oprah's questions were designed to stimulate conversation. Oprah has earned the right to ask such questions, and she is a powerful advocate for those who have been abused. But sadly, this type of thinking by others is often society's way of discounting the complexity of victimization and putting the responsibility on the victim.

We don't want to deal with victims of domestic violence. Or if we are willing to deal with them, we only want to deal with them once and then see that the problem goes away. And when dealing with them once does not solve the problem...we blame them. We demean them. We criticize them. We refer them to other agencies. And often, we end up trying to ignore them. The emergency room doctor wants to refer them to their family physician. The church or synagogue wants the government to deal with them. And when no other professionals are in sight, we have our fallback position—their family should be helping them. It is none of our business. It is not our problem.

Our bias against battered women, in fact, serves us well. It saves us time and energy. We are busy, harried, rushed human beings. We constantly look for a few extra minutes. We regularly try to avoid additional time commitments. So it should come as no surprise that we regularly shortchange battered women and abused men, even if they identify themselves to us. It does not take much to make them go away. And we certainly don't easily welcome them. Why don't we? Why do we welcome them once but not the second, third, or fourth time they seek help? The answer is often unspoken but latent in the hearts of most of us. As a society, we don't want them to come forward. We don't really want to deal with them. Why? Let's be honest! We know what will happen. We have heard the old adage—if you build it, they will come. If we welcome them, we will be deluged. We don't have the resources to deal with the full scope of the problem so we choose to deny it, ignore it, or explain it away.

Most communities and most agencies decide not to build systems that will cause victims, in all forms, to come forward in large numbers. Better to have a complicated intervention system than an extremely accessible one. Better to screen people repeatedly than to simply welcome them all without reservation. Better to stay small and sustainable than to grow large and require substantial resources to maintain our operations. Our bias against battered women is evidenced even in the agencies that care the most for victims and their children.

A number of years ago, I talked to an elected sheriff in the Midwest who did not want to do a public awareness campaign on domestic violence. At first, his excuse was that domestic violence was not a major issue in his community. Within 10 minutes, though, the real reason came through: A public awareness campaign would bring more victims, and more victims would raise the crime statistics in his county! Ignorance was bliss. Ignorance was a chance to brag publicly that since his election, violent crime had dropped 27% in his county. Never mind that the drop in domestic violence cases was likely the result of law enforcement officers failing to take reports, not a dramatic drop in actual violence and abuse in intimate relationships. It was more likely that victims did not feel safe enough to come forward than that the crime was not happening in homes in that community. And law enforcement is not alone. Many agencies come up with many ways to limit the cases they handle and the services they offer.

The bias, however, runs even deeper than simply not wanting to take the time to deal comprehensively with victims of domestic violence. If we are honest, in our heart of hearts, most of us still think there is something wrong with victims of domestic violence. They made poor decisions. They made bad choices. They are weak, unwilling to leave their abusers. Few of us want to help those we believe are unwilling to help themselves. And it is easy to rationalize our distance from those who are victimized: "She made her bed." "She married him!" "She moved in with him." "What does she do to push his buttons?" "If I was living with her, I'd hit her, too."

Over the years, I have heard it all—from friends, co-workers, neighbors, police officers, judges, prosecutors, pastors, and, at times, even advocates. For those who become victims, such bias usually dissipates. But even those who have experienced abuse can sometimes feel no sympathy for victims who are unable to leave quickly after the abuse begins. The reasoning goes, in the quietness of the heart: "If I left after the first or second incident, why can't she?" Irrespective of the reasons for a lack of sympathy and understanding, for the vast majority of Americans who have never been personally victimized, it is indeed a difficult issue to understand.

Our victim blaming is most often a safety mechanism. If victims are stupid, or ignorant, or culpable in some way, our own responsibility for their plight is diminished. We can always feel less social responsibility for the homeless if we can blame them for being homeless. Likewise, we can always feel less responsible for the battered victim if his or her own choices put them in the mess in which they now find themselves. The classic line from *The Burning Bed,* the well-known 1977 Farrah Fawcett movie about a battered woman and her abusive husband rings true even today. When the wife in the movie goes to her mother for help, her mom delivers our bias with a firm tone, declining to help her and, in fact, telling her to go home to her abusive husband: "You made your bed hard, you lie in it." Sadly, that sentiment is alive and well in the hearts of many, even if it is no longer politically correct to say it out loud in our slowly changing culture.

THE QUESTION WE ALL ASK

Beyond the obvious bias against, dislike of, and blame toward the victim, however, is a deeper bias. It is rooted in a question that still permeates our culture—"Why does she stay?" It is *the question*. It has been explained and argued about in books, at conferences, and in personal debates and discussions for years across the country. I talked about it at length in my first book but it deserves additional focus here. *The question* permeates the mind of the law enforcement first responder, the medical first responder, the social worker, the next-door neighbor, and every other person in our culture dealing with battered women. It may not always be voiced but it is always present. *The question* is always just below the surface, even if we never voice it. We read about a victim in the newspaper and we wonder why she stays. It is always present and it is insidious. What is the matter with her? If she really is being victimized, why doesn't she leave?

The bias of "Why does she stay?" often appears in the form of other responses. Instead of asking her why she stays, we say, "You need to leave him." Or we phrase it more as a victim blaming question—"Why don't you just leave?" or "Why don't you protect your children?" or "Why don't you get a restraining order?" Whatever the version of *the question,* though, the underlying pathology is evident. We blame her for what has happened. If she had left, this would not have happened. If she had reported the violence the first time it happened, we would not be dealing with 10 years of complicated abuse patterns. Based on research, the fundamental problem with this approach is obvious. It blames the victim for the violence. Her injuries become her fault. The impact of the violence on the children becomes her fault. Because she stayed, now her children are traumatized and damaged. Because she stayed, the violence has escalated. Because she stayed, she now uses alcohol to self-medicate. Our biased question becomes a large neon sign flashing in her face that says, "This is your fault."

Tragically, when victims are blamed by intervention professionals, or even caring, well-meaning neighbors or family members, they are not more likely to get help. They do not suddenly snap to their senses and break out of the abusive situation they are trapped within. They often turn away from the one blaming them. Sadly, they often return to the abuser in the face of blame. The abuser, after all, blames them for everything. If the intervention professional or the loved one now blames them as well, they see no hope to break the cycle of violence. Without a safe place to seek refuge, a return to the abuser seems the only viable alternative for the victim. If she has to go twenty places to get all the help she needs, it is usually easier to go back home. The abuser is usually happy to have the victim come home and the emotional bond with the abuser is far more powerful than a brief interaction with an acquaintance, friend, or domestic violence professional.

The other troubling aspect of *the question* is the assumption that underlies it. In asking, we assume that if she leaves, the violence will stop and she will be safe. Neither assumption has any basis in reality unless a lot of people work together to help her. Indeed, the research is now incontrovertible that when a victim leaves her abuser, she is actually in greater danger than when she stays.[8] Clearly, this danger does dissipate over time for many victims. But when a victim leaves, the violence does not stop. In fact, "…the most severe violence and the greatest threat of fatality may exist when a battered woman leaves,[9] and this threat may exist for months and even years after she has gone.[10] So our assumption is false. What victims have been saying for years is far more accurate than we understood. When a victim said, "I am scared to death of him, but I am staying with him," we thought she was crazy. Now the truth is confirmed—battered women know *instinctively* what we now know statistically; victims are in more danger when they leave than when they stay with their abusive partners.

The reality of the danger to victims when they try to leave should therefore guide everything we do to help them. We should rethink our deep-seated biases, our words, and our unspoken assumptions. And we should eliminate *the question* from our vocabulary. Never again should we be caught asking "Why does she stay?" unless we understand the complexity of the answer.

Over 10 years ago, domestic violence experts identified fear of her batterer's retaliatory violence as the number two reason a woman stays.[11] The number one reason was she hoped her partner would change.[12] Women in one early study listed fear of violence and other forms of retaliation, along with the following, as the reasons for staying that ring as true today as they did over 25 years ago:

He kept seeking me out and finding me.

I felt other people would die if I left.

He was suicidal; I feared he would come after me.

I have left before and still can't get away from the abuse, threats, and fears.

I remember feeling afraid to go and afraid to stay. The very real fear of revenge is such a powerful deterrent to doing anything....[13]

Can we agree to stop asking victims why they have not left sooner? Let's never ask a victim again why she didn't leave sooner. And let's never let a friend or co-worker utter the words "Why does she stay?" without a firm, clear response from us about the reality of the situation a victim faces in dealing with domestic violence and how difficult it is to leave.

THE WAY TO COMMUNICATE HONOR, RESPECT, AND CARE

If we can be honest about our biases and get educated about our ignorance in understanding family violence, we can deal with the next piece: We need to respect and honor victims of family violence if we are going to help them. Before we can talk about the exciting trend toward more co-located services for victims, we need to understand how to talk to those experiencing family violence. How we treat them and how we talk to them helps us show honor, respect, and care...and lays the foundation for setting up programs and systems to provide services and support.

FIVE SIMPLE THINGS TO SAY TO VICTIMS OF FAMILY VIOLENCE

I have spent a great deal of time with victims and survivors of domestic violence (good idea). My wife and I have housed them (bad idea). We have helped fund housing for them (good idea). I have tried to lecture them (bad idea). They have lectured me (good idea). I have often failed to let them say all they need to say (bad idea). And I have brainstormed with them about options for their lives (good idea). I have chased them down the street while their batterer is hitting them (bad idea). But most importantly, I have decided to accept them and support them—no strings attached (good idea).

Out of those many interactions, I have begun to learn how to talk to victims who come forward. I have also been immensely aided in my steep learning curve by professionals in the field of family violence intervention. Heroic, powerful women like Sarah Buel, Ellen Pence, Barbara Hart, Debby Tucker, and many others have challenged me in how I talk to victims of domestic violence.

Perhaps Sarah Buel, a nationally recognized prosecutor, advocate, trainer, and survivor, mentioned in the Introduction to this book has contributed the most to the five simple statements that should roll off the tongue of every caring person who is talking to a victim of domestic violence. And I credit Sarah with much of the wording behind each of these statements.

They are statements you can use to begin the journey with a victim of domestic violence, once she identifies herself. So let's take a shot at five simple things to say to adult victims of family violence as a starting point.

I am afraid for your safety.

Most victims of domestic violence know when they are in danger.[14] My friend Gavin de Becker, in his New York Times bestseller, *The Gift of Fear*, identified the problem that often occurs with domestic violence victims and others who know instinctively when they are in danger. They ignore their instincts. They let other mental processes overcome their fears. Victims of domestic violence, specifically, deal with so many complex emotions that they do not pay adequate attention to their fears. Many times they have lived with the fear for so long that it is normative. They need to be validated. They need an objective third party to express concern for their safety. They do not need to be blamed. They do not need someone to minimize the past violence or threat of future violence. Victims minimize on their own, without any help from others. They need someone to speak honestly, personally, and lovingly. They need someone to validate the intense fear that obsesses the recesses of their mind but is often buried beneath immediate life needs. They need food and shelter. They need money. Their children are acting out. They need to find a job. They miss their abuser. They love their abuser. They believe he will change and that they can help change him.

When we say, "I am afraid for your safety," we dig through the immediate needs. We reach into the recesses of the victim's mind and find the raw fear that is there. It helps her bring questions that lie dormant to the forefront of her mind. Will he hit me again? Will he escalate the violence next time? Will the injuries be more serious next time? Will he kill me? If someone else is scared for my safety, then maybe my fear is rational. Maybe his apologies are not a guarantee of future safety. The simple fact is that if he has hit in the past, he is likely to hit again. One simple statement can begin many profound and powerful thought processes in the mind of a victim. Coupled with encouragement to talk to a domestic violence professional about her fears, it can be the beginning of planning for her safety. Those thought processes can help her to rationally and thoughtfully, with professional assistance, think through the issues that need to be addressed in order to provide for her own safety.

But helping a victim articulate those fears is still a powerful first step in encouraging her to seek professional help for planning her safety if she chooses to leave. Whether the victim is still with the abuser or has left the abuser, professionally trained advocates now know how to help victims plan for their safety.

The challenge is to connect emotionally with the victim's profound level of fear. Even if we have never been victimized personally, we all understand a victim's fear if we reflect back to some of those scary dreams we had as children or adults. Have you ever had one? Most people have—that dream where someone is after you and you get to a point where you are so scared you cannot scream, you cannot move; you are paralyzed with fear. Put yourself in it. That is what victims of domestic violence feel constantly.

Caring family members and friends should not substitute themselves for experienced domestic violence advocates who know how to help a victim plan for her safety, but we should all know that such safety plans often mean the difference between safety and further violence, between life and death. Safety planning is complex and involved, and should be done in a specialized domestic violence program setting in a shelter, in a prosecutor's office, or in a Center. But it is extremely helpful to know that once a victim starts focusing on her own safety, it is easier to get her to seek the help of trained professionals who can help her to be safe.

I am afraid for the safety of your children.

Working with battered women, and years of research and evaluation have confirmed something that many in the domestic violence movement have known for years: Women are more likely to leave their abusers when they realize the impact of the violence on their children. Battered women do not intentionally put their children in harm's way. They do not intentionally ignore the profound impact on their children. But they minimize the impact. They ignore the impact. They choose to believe their children are resilient and protected from the impact. Those working in the movement now know that is not true. Some children are resilient and do bounce back quickly from witnessing violence, but most children are significantly impacted. Children who witness violence between adults carry it with them for the rest of their lives. And children in domestic violence homes are often physically and sexually abused themselves. So the challenge is to focus the adult victim, usually a woman, on the effect family violence has on her children.

Telling a victim that you fear for the safety of her children is tricky work because a slight, even subtle, variation in this theme of expressing fear for her children's safety can become victim blaming. We can quite unknowingly point the finger at the victim, as we discussed earlier in the chapter. "Why aren't you protecting your kids?" "Do you see what you are doing to your kids by leaving them in this violent situation?" It does not take much. Suddenly, it is her fault. You are not on her side. You see her as a bad mother. You see her as part of the problem. And instantly you have lost an opportunity to build a bridge with someone desperately in need of your help and support.

However, the statement, "I am afraid for the safety of your children," is neutral. It does not blame her. In fact, it likely validates her. Again, at some level, she knows that her children are caught in the cross fire. She knows that her children are experiencing the pain and the trauma. But she does not want to believe it. She is trying to save her marriage. Her children become secondary. She wants them to have a father. She is focused on her primary relationship, and it needs major attention.

But when a caring friend says, "I am afraid for the safety of your children," it focuses her on the honest concern of another for her children's well being. The victim of domestic violence quickly begins to focus there as well. And when she does, her deep love for her children helps her begin to evaluate objectively the costs and benefits of being in an abusive relationship. As she weighs the pros and cons of staying with her abuser or leaving, she begins to factor in what he is doing to her children and what he may still do to them if she stays. Expressing concern for the safety of her children may plant a seed in a victim's mind, even though she has returned to her abuser over and over in the past. It may begin to help her see why she must seek help and why her abuser must be held accountable for his conduct.

It has become clear over the years that victims of domestic violence are more likely to leave when they realize the impact of the violence on their children. Many victims tell us that they did not decide to leave their abuser until they fully understood what it was doing to their children. So, lovingly and carefully helping her to see those impacts without blaming her for them is a very important way to move her toward leaving an abusive relationship.

You do not deserve to be treated like this.

Perhaps the greatest struggle for victims of family violence is the tendency to blame themselves and to believe the abuser's verbal and emotional abuse which, even more powerfully than the violence, demeans them, ridicules them, and puts them down. Counselors, advocates, and therapists working with battered women identify low levels of self-esteem in any clinical assessment. After months, years, and even decades of verbal, emotional, and physical abuse, victims believe they deserve to be treated badly. They must deserve it, or so they reason, or they would not have been treated like this. Indeed, many batterers tell their partners they deserve it. The children too come to think and talk like their father and mother over time.

Whenever you communicate value and inherent worth to a victim of verbal, emotional, and physical abuse, you counteract the poison that has soaked into their lives over many years. The American Psychological Association said many years ago that it takes 11 positive comments to counteract the effects of 1 negative comment. So keep in mind that you have to tell them they don't deserve to be treated like this many, many times given how many times they have been told they do deserve to be treated badly!

There is help available.

Few other messages are as important today for those caught in the web of family violence and relationship abuse. Not only do many victims become isolated and hopeless, but many do not realize how much help is available. Thousands of community organizations and caring professionals exist to deal with the aftermath of family violence. Specialists abound. Police officers and prosecutors are specializing in family violence intervention. Advocates and attorneys are specially trained to meet the needs of family violence victims. Doctors, nurses, therapists, teachers, and even many judges now have significant knowledge and training about issues related to abuse in the home. Pastors, priests, and rabbis are becoming educated and available to help.

There is help available and everyone should be able to deliver that message. Simply offering victims the phone number for the National Domestic Violence Hotline gives them a sense of the help available: (800) 799-SAFE. Memorize it! Then be prepared to offer it to anyone in need. Virtually every community also has a local hotline that you can find in the phone book. You can obtain brochures from the local domestic violence shelter and distribute them in your business, school, or place of worship.[15] Today, in many communities as well you can contact your Family Justice Center and ask for posters or other materials to distribute.[16]

I am here for you no matter what.

Now the platitudes about loving our neighbor and caring for our fellow man end. Now the moment of truth arrives. If we are going to engage in the high calling of caring about the abused and terrorized in homes everywhere, we need to be there for them. We need to deliver the statements here with passion and commitment even if victims choose to return to the abusive situation over and over. When we come in contact with a friend or loved one in need, and offer help and they do not accept it, what are we going to do? When we explain the conduct they are tolerating is a crime and they return to their criminal abuser anyway, what are we going to do? When they tell us to "butt out," what are we going to do?

The right answer for those who want to do the right thing is to deliver this simple message: I am here for you no matter what and whenever you want my help. There should be no judgment. There should be no ultimatums. There should be no emotional or financial manipulation. There should be no victim blaming. The research tells us that many victims of family violence leave five to seven times before they leave for the last time.

Victims are emotionally invested in the abusive relationship. They believe they can change their partners. They believe love can conquer all and that their love can transform evil to good. They are financially committed to the abusive relationship. They, like all of us, want to make their relationship work. They don't want to give up. They want an intact family. They want the violence to stop. They want their partner to get help. But they may not accept the help of outsiders initially. They may leave and return. They may get angry when others try to intervene. They may even view interveners as the enemy. But we must remain available for that moment when they are ready for help. We must remain ready no matter how many times it takes and no matter how many times we have to offer the same words of encouragement.

CONCLUSION

We must overcome our bias against victims of family violence, our unwillingness to deal with them and our tendencies to blame them. And we need to show them respect and honor before we try to help them.

If you have read the Introduction and now Chapter 1, you are definitely ready to help change the world! We only need to add one more piece to this before we get into the "meat" of the co-located services concept. The next chapter focuses on the history of the domestic violence movement and is critical to successful Centers in the future because it recognizes where Family Justice Centers came from and what has happened in the history of the domestic violence movement that has produced our dream for providing more and more services under one roof.

NOTES

1   The largest studies done at the Nampa Family Justice Center (Nampa, ID) and at the San Diego Family Justice Center (San Diego, CA) confirm what is simple common sense. If we all work together in one place, victims feel more supported , feel safer (and are safer), and feel more able to handle their lives and the issues in their lives surrounding violence. (See www.familyjusticecenter. org/ResourceLibrary for more information on the outcome studies that have been done. Join as a Member and then go to Outcome Data).

2   Eleanor Lyon, Shannon Lane, Anne Menard, "Meeting Survivors' Needs: A Multi-State Study of Domestic Violence Shelter Experiences," (2008). To view a copy of the full report, go to: http://new.vawnet.org/Assoc_Files_VAWnet/ MeetingSurvivorsNeeds-FullReport.pdf.

3   Elaine Weiss, *Family and Friends Guide to Domestic Violence,* Volcano Press, Volcano, CA, 2003.

4   Del Martin, *Battered Wives.* Volcano Press. Volcano, California, 1976.

5   Susan Schecter, *Women and Male Violence: The Visions and Struggles of the Battered Women's Movement,* South End Press, 1982, p.23-24.

6   Id.

7   Gavin DeBecker, *The Gift of Fear,* Little, Brown and Co., Boston, 1997.

8   Dr. Jacquelyn Campbell's research at Johns Hopkins University and the compilation of research that has helped shape the Danger Assessment Tool (www. dangerassessment.com) used to evaluate the risk of lethality in domestic violence cases has consistently demonstrated that 70-75% of all women who are victims of domestic violence homicide were leaving or attempting to leave the relationship at the time of their death.

9   M. Mahoney, "Legal Images of Battered Women: Redefining the Issue of Separation," *Michigan Law Review* 30, 1991, 97-102.

   J. Ptacek, "The Tactics of Men Who Batter: Testimony From Women Seeking Restraining Orders," in A. Cardarelli (Ed.), *Violence Between Intimate Partners: Patterns, Causes and Effects,* Allyn and Bacon, Boston, 1997, pp. 104-23.

10 M. Wilson and M. Daly, "Spousal Homicide Risk and Estrangement," *Violence and Victims,* 1993, 9: 3-16.

11 Ola W. Barnett and Alyce D. La Violette. *It Could Happen to Anyone: Why Battered Women Stay,* Sage Publications, Thousand Oaks, CA, 1993, p. 48.

12 Ibid, p. 48-9.

13 Ibid.

14 H. Eigenberg, "Woman Battering in the United States: Till Death Do Us Part," Chapter Three, *Explaining Battering* Waveland Press, Inc., Long Grove, IL, 2001, p. 134.

15 *A Community Checklist: Important Steps To End Violence Against Women,* United

States Department of Justice, Advisory Council on Violence Against Women, 1995.

16 Go to www.familyjusticecenter.org to see a listing of all operating or developing Family Justice Centers or similar co-located, multi-agency service centers in the United States.

CHAPTER TWO

Knowing Where We Came from, and How We Need to Evolve

A number of years ago, I was speaking at a conference in the Midwest where a recently elected Sheriff decided to hold a press conference at noon to brag about all the great work he was doing to hold abusers accountable, help victims, and reduce family violence. He was articulate, powerful, and persuasive. But as I listened to him, all I could think of was his arrogance. He was the elected Mr. Know It All. As I listened, I looked around the room and it got even more painful. The shelter director was there and not recognized or even allowed to speak. Multiple advocates from community-based agencies were there and not introduced or allowed to speak. No survivor ever came to the podium during his press conference. As he talked on and on, it became clear that he thought he invented the domestic violence movement in his county. He was the leader, he was the reason people were being served, and he was the reason that almost anything good was happening in that community. Then, he made a terrible mistake. He invited me to the podium and gave me the microphone... Of course I will never be invited back to that county. I will never have dinner and drinks with the Sheriff. He won't send me a holiday card or recommend me to others for speaking engagements. Because I stepped to the microphone and told the audience and the media the history of the domestic violence movement in America! I introduced the shelter director and asked her to come up and speak. I reminded everyone that we are products of courageous feminist women who have come before us. We are indebted to many that have lost their lives, to many that have shared their stories, and to many that shaped a social change movement in this country long before we were on the scene. Toward the end of my last speech ever to be given in that community...I apologized for not honoring our past enough, for not recognizing that the criminal justice system was late to this work, and I apologized for the many mistakes we had made when we arrested battered women, threatened to take their children away, failed to hold their abusers accountable, and failed to advocate for the necessary resources to properly address the overwhelming needs of victims and their children. I closed my remarks with a commitment to keep learning and keep listening as we sought to do a better job of stopping abusers and helping victims. It was the last speech that Mr. Know It All would ever invite me to give but it was worth it.

We cannot know where to go until we have reviewed where we have been and understood where we came from. And we cannot understand the need to change direction until we fully understand the direction we are going. One of my heroes, Abraham Lincoln, said it more eloquently over 150 years ago. In his "A House Divided" speech in 1858 delivered before the Republican State Convention of Illinois, Lincoln said, "If we could first know where we are, and whither we are tending, we could better judge what to do, and how to do it." This book is about a trend toward more comprehensive services for victims of violence and abuse that was launched by the domestic violence movement in this country. To understand where that "trend" should go, we should understand where we came from and where we are now.

Books have been written about the history of the domestic violence movement.[1] In our first book, I included a short chapter on the history of the domestic violence movement.[2] Mindful of the complexity of this history, let's just look at a very brief history of where we've come from to help us understand why Family Justice Centers and other types of co-located service models are now developing and expanding in so many communities.

For thousands of years we have tolerated violence against women. And for thousands of years family violence has been documented. The problem is as old as Cain and Abel. It has been ignored, condoned, and sometimes even glorified. Throughout the centuries, violence in intimate relationships has been normative in most cultures around the world. No one did anything about it until the last few hundred years. And only in the last 50 years, with the development of the battered women's movement, has any real progress been made. In the 1960s and 1970s, the battered women's movement evolved out of the women's movement and focused on providing shelter to women and their children fleeing abusive and violent men.

In 1982, Susan Schecter did an excellent job of looking at the history of the domestic violence movement in the 1960s and 1970s.[3] But the history goes back much further than the modern development of the battered women's movement.[4] In 1868, the legal doctrine of *family privacy* was articulated by courts in North Carolina and across the country with the following statement: "However great are the evils of ill temper, quarrels, and even personal conflicts inflicting only temporary pain, they are not comparable with the evils which would result from raising the curtain and exposing to public curiosity and criticism the nursery and the bed chamber."[5]

Ellen Pence cites research looking back as early as 1640 for the genesis of the struggle against *wife beating* and the call for the government to play a role in providing protection for abused women.[6] Pence writes:

> The suffrage and progressive social reform movements of the late 19th century produced legislative changes, ending more than 200 years of regulating wife beating, and criminalized the practice regardless of the woman's behavior. By 1911, laws forbidding wife beating had been passed in every state. Because no infrastructure of local efforts existed to advocate for implementation of the new laws, they were noted in law books and shelved until 70 years later,

when the next wave of feminism gained momentum and activists insisted on their enforcement.[7]

In the 1960s, the women's movement began to call on male-dominated institutions throughout our culture to start paying attention to violence against women. Violence in intimate relationships was only one of many issues addressed by the women's movement, but it soon became a very identifiable movement in and of itself. The focus on culturally acceptable violence against women was new in the 1960s. Indeed, one of the first major legal decisions in America to address the new awareness of the issue was not published until 1964 when the North Carolina Supreme Court said it was better to "forgive and forget," but acknowledged the reality that some violence in the home had to be criminalized when it rose to such a level that serious injury or death occurred.[8]

In the 1970s, the battered women's movement began to grow out of the much larger women's movement and included the anti-rape movement. The battered women's movement was a loosely arranged group of survivors of family violence and feminist advocates who began to organize survivors into an identifiable group of activists. The movement grew slowly at first, but then more quickly as private shelters and privately funded social service programs developed. Although it was made up primarily of women, small numbers of progressive men supported the movement even in the late 1970s and early 1980s. And though the movement was distinct from other powerful social change movements developing in America, it found common allies in the civil rights movement and later in the child abuse movement.

In the 1980s, feminist advocates began demanding legal protections for battered women. Del Martin's seminal book, published in 1976, became a clarion call for caring people across America to step forward and act to stop family violence.[9] Class-action and individual lawsuits were filed by victims and survivors attempting to treat violence against women as a civil rights issue under state and federal law. One of the most famous lawsuits was litigated and became a published court decision in 1983 when Tracy Thurman successfully sued the City of Torrington, Connecticut, for violating her civil rights by failing to protect her from her violent and abusive husband, Buck Thurman.[10] As Joan Zorza points out, the effect of this one case was dramatic, not only because a federal jury awarded Tracy and her son $2.3 million, but it "was widely reported in popular press and in academic journals. It graphically confirmed the extreme financial penalty that could be imposed on police departments when they abjectly fail to perform their duties. In addition, it confirmed that in appropriate cases these massive liability awards would be upheld."[11]

The Tracy Thurman story became a movie and educated many about the terror and trauma of domestic violence. Many individual victims began using civil litigation to demand monetary compensation from law enforcement agencies that failed to protect them from their abusers. Mandatory arrest laws, restraining order laws, pro-prosecution policies, and a host of legal mandates came forward in legislatures across the country. Specialized police officers, advocates, and prosecutors sprang up in jurisdictions across the nation as we began to realize the difficulty of dealing with domestic violence cases in the criminal justice system.

In 1984, then-Attorney General Edwin Meese created the first national task force on domestic violence issues with the support of President Ronald Reagan. For the first time, the federal government looked at the broad nature of family violence issues. Still today, the *Task Force Report* is an excellent primer on the complex history of family violence issues in America. It also yielded a powerful set of recommendations that helped launch many initiatives in the mid-1980s.

As the newly established domestic violence intervention movement developed political power, more and more policy makers and elected officials began to advocate for resources, legislation, and policy changes related to America's response to violence in the home. Nationally and internationally, more and more attention was being given to the issue of domestic violence.

In the 1990s, the mainstreaming of a feminist view of domestic violence (violence as a power and control behavior exercised through male privilege) continued. Specially trained police officers, prosecutors, and judges, all products of the feminist movement, began advocating their views within the criminal justice system itself. In 1991, the National College of District Attorneys held its first ever national conference on the prosecution of domestic violence. Judges, prosecutors, police officers, and advocates from across the country came together for the first time.

Prosecutors attending the first and subsequent conferences of the National College of District Attorneys learned how to prosecute cases even if the victim did not want to "press charges." Evidence-based prosecution, first advocated by law enforcement agencies in Minnesota in the early 1980s, was endorsed by the National College of District Attorneys as the best approach to victim safety and abuser accountability. Simply put, evidence-based prosecution was the strategy to prosecute a batterer even if the victim refused to press charges or testify. Jurisdictions such as San Diego, California, Quincy, Massachusetts, and Baltimore, Maryland, led the way in training prosecutors in newly developed prosecution techniques. For the first time anywhere in America, the responsibility for law enforcement intervention in family violence cases was slowly removed from the shoulders of victims and placed squarely on the criminal justice system itself. Advocates, police officers, prosecutors, and judges began working together cooperatively to develop coordinated approaches to deal with the long-neglected crime of domestic violence. While controversy swirled around so-called "mandatory arrest" laws and "no-drop" prosecution policies, more and more jurisdictions began treating domestic violence as seriously as any other major crime.

Though the issue remains somewhat controversial in some jurisdictions, the thesis of aggressive prosecution with or without victim participation is simple. If we don't ask victims of other serious crimes if they want to press charges, why should we ask domestic violence victims? If someone robs a bank, no one asks the bank teller if she wants to press charges. Why? Because bank robbery has been defined as a serious crime in this country and bank robbers get held accountable whether or not the teller in the bank wants to testify, or "prosecute"! Slowly, jurisdictions began applying the same principle to both misdemeanor and felony domestic violence cases.

As the change process evolved, judges from across the country began joining in the criminal justice focus on domestic violence. In 1992, the first-ever National Judges Conference on Domestic Violence was funded by the State Justice Institute and organized by the National Council of Juvenile and Family Court Judges. The Chief Justice of each state Supreme Court named a delegation that attended the conference and worked on statewide plans to train judges, educate court personnel, and revise court policies and procedures to better protect the rights of domestic violence victims. The conference, held in San Francisco, California, became a catalyst for organizing efforts in court systems across the nation and inspired many of the specialized domestic violence courts that have developed.

Without question, the 1990s saw an ongoing expansion of laws related to domestic violence, child custody issues, child support issues, and other related legal issues that impact families torn apart by violence. Policy-based legislation was only one part of the national legislative focus. The first major federal funding for domestic violence initiatives in American history finally occurred in 1994. The Violence Against Women Act (VAWA) became a landmark piece of legislation. Passed by Congress and signed by President Bill Clinton, VAWA created federal criminal offenses related to domestic violence,[12] mandated legal protections for battered women,[13] and authorized funding for shelters, tribal communities, law enforcement agencies, prosecutors, and a variety of intervention initiatives in every state. VAWA was a far-reaching, historic, bipartisan step forward in the effort in the United States. Within a similar time frame, laws were being passed and funding was being made available in Canada, Australia, and many other countries in the Western world.

THE O.J. SIMPSON CASE

In June 1994, the O.J. Simpson case focused America, and much of the Western world, on domestic violence issues as never before.

International, national, and local media became captivated by the terror and tragedy of domestic violence. As the case developed and later went to trial, it was covered world-wide. Simpson's acquittal in the criminal case, though stunning to many, did nothing to dampen the public fervor to seek justice for victims of family violence.

The media saturation about the O.J. Simpson case caused widespread public awareness. In 1996, *Newsweek* reported that 96% of Americans deemed domestic violence to be a major social problem in need of attention.[14] More laws were passed, more specialized services were created, and more funding was allocated as public interest skyrocketed. The chilling 911 tapes and other evidence of prior violence by O.J. Simpson that preceded Nicole Brown Simpson's murder caused many to question whether the Los Angeles intervention system had failed to protect Nicole when she was in obvious danger. ABC, NBC, CBS, CNN, Court TV, and other networks produced hundreds of stories on issues surrounding family violence. Print media as well devoted thousands of column inches to telling the stories of domestic violence victims, abusers, and system responses across the country.

It is fair to say that during the 1990s, America focused on domestic violence issues as never before. Task forces formed in local communities and at the state and federal level. Arrest and prosecution became standard procedure in family violence incidents. Counseling and support groups for victims proliferated. Batterer intervention programs multiplied across the country. More specialized resources were devoted to family violence than at any time in our history. And some of the first major public awareness campaigns were launched at the local, state, and national level.

The result of this major focus on family violence was predictable. Mandatory arrest and pro-prosecution policies deluged the criminal justice system with domestic violence cases. Court dockets became clogged and personal attention to individual cases was often sacrificed in favor of "one-size-fits-all" policies for arrest, prosecution, probation, and counseling. Filing policies were refined to find reasons not to file charges, cases were reduced to lesser offensives to relieve jail overcrowding, and the criminal and civil justice systems adapted to survive the massive shift from ignoring family violence to viewing criminal justice as a major part of the solution.

Supporters and opponents of the burgeoning intervention movement could be found throughout the media and popular culture. Many men decried the criminalization of domestic violence as "male bashing." Backlash movements developed as more and more fathers began losing child custody rights in the wake of domestic violence incidents and subsequent divorce actions. Screening for, and analysis of, domestic violence issues became commonplace in divorce actions, medical venues, and employment situations.

Within 20 years, the civil and criminal justice systems in America went from seeing few, if any, domestic violence cases to seeing hundreds of thousands across the country. Law enforcement agencies went from briefly responding to family violence calls and leaving without writing reports or taking action to arresting many offenders and conducting on-scene investigations to facilitate prosecution. The hidden crime was hidden no more. The silent victims were silent no more. And America was, at long last, talking about the carnage of family violence. The dirty little family secret was coming out of the closet. Just as sexual assault in the late 1970s and child abuse in the 1980s, domestic violence was now front and center in the late 1990s. In many ways, the culmination of over a century of social change—the power of the domestic violence movement—was being felt at every level of society.[15]

During this profound period of social change, the battered women's movement also worked to recruit public policy makers, elected officials, doctors, nurses, attorneys, business leaders, and many others in the struggle to stop violence against women. This powerful social change movement resulted in the creation of more resources to help victims and their children than at any other time in human history. The efforts of the battered women's movement to reach out to many different systems in the social change journey in the 1980s and 1990s to stop family violence has resulted in three major changes that have laid the ground work for the Family Justice Center movement and greater co-located services.

First, the effort to reach out to the criminal justice system, the civil justice system, the medical profession, the child welfare system, and the faith community has invited many diverse entities, value systems, intervention approaches, and world views to the human rights struggle against intimate partner violence. They are not all women. They are not all feminists. And they don't all share the same understanding of family violence! But they are all now pursuing the goal of addressing family violence with their own policies, programs, values, and approaches. The list of entities now aware of family violence issues and the relationship of family violence to child abuse, elder abuse, human trafficking, juvenile delinquency, adult criminal conduct (for all crimes), gang violence, homelessness, mental health issues, offender re-entry, and other social ills is a stunningly long list!

Second, the success of the movement has produced more money and more resources for programs that help victims and their children at the local, state, and federal level in the U.S. and in many countries around the world than ever before. The money is still far from adequate but there are more resources devoted to the issue around the globe today than at any time. Thirty years ago there was nothing but a smattering of domestic violence shelters and other types of community-based programs in local communities. Today, there are programs operating out of thousands of non-profits, local government agencies, state and federal agencies in the United States, and around the world.

Third, related to the first two, the result of recruiting so many institutions, disciplines, systems, and entities coupled with the increase in resources at so many levels has *created many, many places and many, many systems where victims have to go to get help in their communities!*

Greater understanding has helped us realize as well all the services that are necessary to truly offer criminal, civil, and economic justice to victims of family violence. Research has also helped us understand that collaboration is the best approach for seeking to prevent family violence before it happens as well as seeking to intervene effectively when it does happen.[16] We saw it coming many years ago when we started developing "coordinated community response" models to address domestic violence even in the early 1990's.

The National District Attorneys Association recently hosted an Institute on the prosecution of domestic violence cases which included a panel entitled "CCRs, MDTs, and FJCs: Oh My!" The panel was an excellent overview of the history of the collaborative work which has evolved out of the involvement of police officers, prosecutors, and judges over the last 20 years in the United States. It highlighted the benefits of many different models that help the criminal justice system address the issues discussed above. Judge Carl Ashley, Milwaukee County Circuit Court Judge, explained how the Milwaukee courts have been looking at coordinated community response and encouraging all the public and private agencies to coordinate their work for over 25 years. He explained how the vision had evolved from a set of relationships to coordinated policies and procedures and, most recently, to planning for a Family Justice Center called the Family Peace Center.[17]

In the same panel discussion, Kay Wallace, a criminal justice analyst in Loudoun County, Virginia shared how Loudoun County had pursued a coordinated community response by developing specialized units and teams in many agencies, organized a Domestic Abuse Response Team, created a countywide coordinating council, and developed a model for interaction though they have never gone to a co-located services model. Tonya Riddell from the Domestic Violence Prosecution Center in Clark County, Washington presented on their model for addressing the challenges over the last decade described in this chapter. Clark County has co-located professionals but only primarily systems-based professionals—cops, prosecutors, and, system-based victim-witness advocates that work for government agencies. But her presentation helped demonstrate the power of co-location even without community-based agency partners. Tonya shared how they conducted multi-disciplinary team meetings to discuss cases. Her presentation helped show the power of co-location when she shared how just having the public agencies together had produced a conversation in a bathroom between women working on the same case that resulted in the team keeping an offender from getting out of jail when they all realized what was happening on the case and raced to court to raise his bail. An MDT in a bathroom because of co-location!

Finally, three of the us on the panel discussion described our work in Family Justice Centers—Mary Claire Landry from New Orleans, Casey Bates from Alameda County, and me from San Diego—and you could see how only co-location fully addresses these issues from the victim's perspective. The victim still experiences many, many places she has to go for help until everyone comes together and co-locates services in one place.

No matter how many policies, protocols, and procedures we create, no matter how well we work together in multi-disciplinary teams or case review meetings, we still have far too many places for victims to go in order to get the help they need. It is has been true and still is true in most communities—rural, suburban, and urban.

TOO MANY PLACES TO GO FOR HELP

The picture on why we need to co-locate services and why it is better if victims can go one place instead of many comes into focus relatively quickly as you understand just how many places victims have to go. They are becoming victims of our own success. Today, there are millions of victims, women and men, trying to go from agency to agency and program to program to find everything they need.

And we keep adding agencies and programs across the country and in local communities to help victims of domestic violence and their children.[18] We keep asking more agencies, more businesses, and more segments of society to join us. And as they have stepped up, we have added to the "maze" that victims must navigate! The business community, the medical community, the law enforcement community, and the court system have all started new initiatives, including agencies that traditionally did not work with domestic violence victims.

Employment programs, colleges, law schools, medical schools, churches, the military, schools, animal shelters, service clubs, and other agencies have begun developing programs to help victims and their children. Though many communities initially focused on law enforcement intervention, expanded opportunities to support victims of domestic violence are now evident throughout society. We have seen it coming for awhile. As more and more local, state, and federal entities began funding services in the late 1980s and the 1990s, it became clear that the list of services was growing very long, particularly in suburban and urban communities. But today the list of services and service providers is longer than ever!

The challenges created by the proliferation of programs were identified and regularly addressed in the domestic violence movement through the concept of coordinated community response.[19] The sexual assault movement and the child advocacy movement also promoted the concept of coordinated community response as the solution to coordinating agencies.[20] Task forces and coordinating councils were promoted by many in the domestic violence movement as the solution to the coordination problems.[21] Today, coordinated community response is the state of the art term to describe how communities and all agencies and entities in a community should work together. Tremendous thinking has gone into this including excellent resources on how to develop a coordinated community response.[22]

Though the problem has been identified, most of our problem-solving efforts in arenas such as task forces or coordinating councils are still system-centered, not victim-centered.[23] Though much has been studied and written about addressing the system challenges, not enough people have spent the time to figure out how many places victims need to go for help as we continue to expand the number of new programs offering services to those in need and continue to try to coordinate all those services. San Diego was one of the first places in America to evaluate this aspect of the problem and it is part of the

I have spent my adult life refusing to allow the abuse I suffered to define me as a human being. That was something that I felt I could control. I was ordered by the court in 1988 to volunteer on behalf of victims of domestic violence. At the time there were no programs like the Nampa Family Justice Center. I was on my own. No counseling, no guidance, no nothing. I felt abused by the system. How could I possibly do one more thing? It took everything I had just to keep going. I had two little girls, ages 1 ½ and 2 ½, no job, no money, and no home. I put my head down and went to work. I worked three jobs, raised my children and tried to forget. My girls have now grown to become educated, passionate, and successful women. I remarried and have two more sweet children, a business, and time to volunteer. As President now of the Foundation for the Family Justice Center, I don't want to admit that the abuse does define me. I don't want to be a victim but I am even today. What does a victim look like? Is it an executive headed to work in a Mercedes Benz? Or a child on a playground with perfect pigtails? Can you see me? If you can't see me, you can't help me. I am embarrassed by this part of my past. As a victim of domestic violence, I feel that somehow on some level I either deserved or contributed to the abuse that was perpetrated on me. Even now, twenty five years later. The victim in me still lurks in the shadows but the survivor in me knows better. Ultimately, the abuse, my survival, my failures and my successes are all part of my story and really it is my story and what I do with it that ultimately defines me. It is my hope that with the assistance of Family Justice Centers that victims will get the help and support they need. That they will be able to go forward after this type of life changing experience with a lighter heart, knowing that we as a community, all support them and we are all together in helping them.

Cory Aguilar, President
Nampa Family Justice Center Foundation

reason San Diego began to point the way toward Family Justice Centers for other communities.

VICTIMS ARE BECOMING VICTIMS OF OUR OWN SUCCESS

San Diego and many other communities saw the proliferation of services coming long before we officially opened the Family Justice Center. Some domestic violence shelters too saw it coming as they added counseling, legal services, child care, and other services in the 1980's and 1990's. In San Diego, we started co-locating services in the prosecutor's office in 1990 with the support of two local shelters.

We had advocates, civil legal service providers, police officers, prosecutors, victim-witness personnel, and child trauma specialists from Children's Hospital all co-located in the City Attorney's Domestic Violence Unit in an effort to avoid the re-victimization of victims by sending them from agency to agency and place to place.[24]

But we really did not see the gravity of the problem of "too many places go to" until 2000, when, using principles developed by Ellen Pence and her team in Duluth, we created a type of "community safety audit" in San Diego to analyze the system we had created to help domestic violence victims and their children. We spent a number of months talking to victims and survivors and reviewed the list of agencies then being provided by the San Diego Police Department to victims at the scene of each reported domestic violence incident. The

We've seen Family Justice Centers stumble and fall when a single entity tries to own it and control it, and tell others how to do it. It's too complex; too many moving parts. All key partners need to be involved and it takes a very unique process to help a community come together to create a Center.

I've helped launch Centers, from California to Amman Jordan, and each time we began by asking partners to step into the future and to imagine… "our Center—open, successful, making a difference". We asked them to step out on faith, suspend doubts and old feuds, and consider what could be; how it might work, and how services in a single location instead of 32 locations could make life better, safer, and hope-filled for victims and their children.

The simple act of providing partners with the opportunity to "dream big" opens a space for listening to ideas from each partner's perspective. Then, when all the ideas have been collected, intuitively, they begin to see new possibilities and a larger solution emerges. And that's the key. No one person has the solution…we all do, but we have to work together to discover it and to make it work.

The shared vision becomes the cornerstone for the rest of the process; we ask what we are afraid of, what will it take, who's missing…but we have to keep coming back together to work things out, solve problems, learn, admit mistakes—we have to work together. Victims can't do it alone and neither can we.

Judi Adams, Strategic Planner and co-author of *The Big Girls Club*

question was posed: How many places does a victim have to go to get all the help she/he needs in San Diego?

Within a few months, we were able to identify 32 different agencies that had services for victims of domestic violence. And few of those agencies were in the same place! Creating a coordinated community response, developing a task force, creating a host of specialized units to provide services to victims had not solved the problem; we had made it worse.

More and more communities are now studying how many places their victims need to go to get help. Rural communities are reporting that their victims need to go to five to seven places, suburban communities are reporting 15 to 20 agencies where victims need to travel, and metropolitan communities are finding an even larger number of places where their victims need to go to get help, including medical services, counseling services for themselves, counseling services for their children, safety planning, legal services, law enforcement assistance, spiritual support, job training, financial/credit counseling, shelter services, criminal prosecution assistance, home security advice, transportation assistance, court involvement—and the list goes on. But suburban communities can have a list as long as San Diego. In 2010, in Shasta County, California, the planning team for the Shasta County Family Justice Center identified 32 different places in their small county of 185,000 people where victims needed to go for help.[25] Metropolitan communities can even have a longer list. In Brooklyn, New York, in the planning for their first Family Justice Center, Mayor Bloomberg's planning team identified 64 partner agencies that needed to collaborate in their Center![26]

Many looking at this issue for the first time, who do not work in the domestic violence field, would think: "Surely there must be one agency that already provides all this help." Battered women's shelters, after all, have been moving down this road toward multidisciplinary services for their clients for years. But the reality is clear. Even the most well-funded shelters only have a few of the services their clients really need. Shelter victims wanting help may get short-term housing and support groups or counseling at the shelter, but generally must go elsewhere for other services. Rarely is a full-service employment training operation available in a shelter. Victims need legal assistance including restraining orders, divorce assistance, and immigration law advice. But even if the shelter has a legal advisor on-site for these diverse needs, a victim still must go to court to get a restraining order, not to mention the myriad other legal assistance she needs.

And what if the victim needs law enforcement assistance? Only a handful of shelters in the country have police officers and prosecutors available at the shelter. It gets even more complicated when a community has five to 10 law enforcement agencies in one county or parish and perhaps both a county prosecutor's office and a city prosecutor's office. No existing agency in the country provided access to all such service providers from a single location in 1998.

To be sure, some communities went down the road toward co-located services.[27] A few communities had police officers and prosecutors housed together. Some shelters had five to six disciplines represented in a single location. But in most places, victims traveled from place to place to place to tell their story over and over in an attempt to get the help they needed.

If a victim needed medical help, she would go to a hospital emergency room. If she needed follow-up assistance, she would go to her primary care doctor (if she had one). If she wanted to go to a battered women's shelter but needed to have her pets cared for, she had to find someone to take her pets. If her children were actually physically abused, they would end up in the child protective system, and a whole new set of agencies would be necessary. If the victim had been sexually assaulted, sexual assault protocols would kick in, and a long list of agencies and services would be added to the referral sheet handed to her by well-meaning professionals.

Are you tired yet? Getting dizzy? If you are a survivor reading this, you know how difficult it was in San Diego—and still is in most communities—to find everything you needed on a map, let alone actually going to those locations. And what if you don't have a car? What if public transportation is your only access to such services? What if the agency you need is not on a bus route?

By 1998, we could not deny the reality. We had created a gauntlet for victims of domestic violence and their children. At one end of their journey was the violence and abuse; at the other end was supposed to be safety and healing. But in between, we made them run through a nightmarish, confusing obstacle course of agencies. To fit our policies, protocols, and procedures, we were sending victims careening back and forth across the community for help. To make it convenient for our bureaucratic systems to provide services, we were demanding almost superhuman tenacity and endurance from victims. The more I think about it, the more dumbfounded I get. We had created a system for the convenience of system professionals, not for the convenience of victims and their children.

So what happened to our victims in San Diego when we put them through the gauntlet? It was no different than much of the rest of the country still is today. Victims don't make it through the system. They might get to a police department, but they never make it to the

The concept of co-location is not a new one for domestic violence shelters who have worked collaboratively for years to meet the multiple needs of the victims/survivors we serve. Now that the Family Justice Center movement is expanding and communities everywhere are looking more closely at the benefits of and need for wraparound, co-located services, it is a fantastic opportunity for local shelters and domestic violence service providers to better serve the needs of our clients as well as more easily engage those clients who may not come to us as a first option. Domestic violence providers and shelters have a responsibility to the people we serve to stay involved, reach out, and participate in the journey. Police, prosecutors, civil attorneys, and medical professionals want to better support and help the survivors who are served in shelters and those survivors/victims often need other professionals to meet their multiple needs. In Salt Lake City, the YWCA has taken the lead in designing our co-located services model and we are developing it in tandem with our other programs including crisis shelter and transitional housing. For us, the FJC model adds to our capacity to serve more victims/survivors in a holistic, client-centered model in our community. When shelters are involved, co-location becomes even more powerful! We hope others will join our vision!

Asha Parekh
Director, Salt Lake Area Family Justice Center
Former Director, YWCA Domestic Violence Shelter

prosecutor's office. They might spend a few days in a shelter, but they never make it to the restraining order clinic. Most of our victims were returning to their abusers without comprehensive intervention ever occurring and most victims still today around the United States are ending up in the same situation.

We need to keep evolving. We need to keep thinking. We are all indebted to the battered women's movement for the work over the last 40 years. We should never forget where we have come from. We should keep listening to the leaders of the movement, keep engaging them in all we do, and keep ensuring that our work is not inconsistent with all they have learned in the early stages of this modern social change movement.

But there is more to be done now. We have identified male victimization as an issue we must also address. We have realized that many women and men who are victims don't come into our systems through domestic violence shelters. In fact, most victims never go to a domestic violence shelter. Most community members and business leaders never have any involvement with their local domestic violence shelter or community-based non-profit agency working on family violence issues. There are now hundreds of potential entry points in communities across the United States and around the world where victims are either identified or disclose for the first time. Children may disclose before their parents which generates a totally different response from the system than if a mother or father come forward to seek help.

This book focuses on one piece of the "long haul ahead." It focuses on the effort to address the many, many places that victims must now

When a Family Justice Center is developed with strong leadership and partnerships with local domestic violence programs, it can be a win-win for survivors and the community. The movement against domestic and sexual violence has come a long way, but we all know there is still a long haul ahead. Communities must come together to change society's tolerance for abuse and provide comprehensive, life-saving services to survivors.

Sue Else, President
National Network to End Domestic Violence

go. The Family Justice Center movement as we will see is just one so-lution, one "evolution point", and one promising practice for keeping the effort to stop family violence moving forward in this country and around the world. But it is an important piece of dreaming big. As the book moves forward, you will start to see more and more "text boxes" with quotes from Family Justice Center clients and professionals who have worked at Centers. They tell the story even better than the book itself of why Family Justice Centers are needed, why they hold great promise for bringing communities together, and why they can be far more effective in meeting a victim's needs than referring the victim from place to place and agency to agency when they seek help.

WHERE TO NOW?

In the face of this history and the challenges it has created for victims and their children, let's now look at the Family Justice Center concept. Let's understand it. Let's see how it works. Let's understand what happens when it works well, when it works poorly, and when it does not work at all! In Chapter 3, we will lay out the vision and give you a sense of how the model works, why it works, and why victims appreciate it so much. In Chapter 4, we will look at why not all com-munities are ready to pursue co-location. In Chapter 5, we will look at why co-location is cost-effective. In Chapter 6, we will look at the exciting innovations and programs that tend to evolve in co-located service models. In Chapter 7, we will look at the greatest challenge in collaborative service models—effective leadership. In Chapter 8, we will look at the challenges that co-located service models must address. In Chapter 9, we will look at why the model can work in many places around the world. And in Chapter 10, we will close with some reflections on the future of Family Justice Centers and other co-located, coordinated community response approaches to addressing family violence.

CONCLUSION

We are all products of the battered women's movement. We need to respect the powerful progress it has made and the issues and opportunities that its progress has created. The Family Justice Center vision, informed by over 40 years of advocacy by the domestic violence movement for coordinated community response and informed police response, is intended to be a personal and corporate call to action in the future, even as we remember the past. The Family Justice Center vision can help women and men who are victims of abuse. This book is a call to grab hold of a vision that can move this country forward in breaking the cycle of family violence.

NOTES

1   Susan Schecter, *Women and Male Violence: The Visions and Struggles of the Battered Women's Movement*, South End Press, Cambridge, MA, 1982. This book is an excellent look at the history of the domestic violence movement in the 1960s and 1970s.

2   Gwinn, Strack, *Hope for Hurting Families: Creating Family Justice Centers Across America* (Volcano Press 2006), Chapter 2, "Looking Back Before We Look Forward", pp. 23-35.

3   Susan Schecter, *Women and Male Violence: The Visions and Struggles of the Battered Women's Movement*, South End Press, Cambridge, MA, 1982.

4   Elizabeth Pleck, *Domestic Tyranny: The Making of Social Policy Against Family Violence From Colonial Times to the Present*, 1987, pp 3-13. [Citing to the Puritans of Massachusetts Bay Colony being the first to pass laws against family violence during the 1870s.]

5   North Carolina Family Privacy Doctrine, "Breaking the Cycle: A Coordinated Community Response to Domestic Violence." Cited in *Coordinated Community Responses to Family Violence*," presentation by Casey Gwinn. June 1992. Available at www.familyjusticecenter.org/library.

6   Ellen Pence and Melanie Shepard, *Coordinating Community Responses to Domestic Violence: Lessons From Duluth and Beyond*, Sage Publications. Thousand Oaks, CA, 1999, pp. 5-6.

7   Ibid., p. 6. Citing R.E. Dobash and R.P. Dobash, *Women, Violence, and Social Change*, Routledge Kegan Paul, New York, 1992.

8   State v. Oliver, 70 N.C. 44 (1874). See also State v. Rhodes, 61 N.C. 453, 459 (Phil. Law 1868). ["It will be observed that the ground upon which we have put this decision is not that the husband has the right to whip his wife much or little, but that we will not interfere with family government in trifling cases.... We will not inflict upon society the greater evil of raising the curtain upon domestic privacy, to punish the lesser evil of trifling violence."]

9   Del Martin, *Battered Wives*, Volcano Press. Volcano, CA, 1976.

10 Thurman v. City of Torrington. Conn., 595 F. Supp. 1521 (DC 1984).

11 Joan Zorza. "The Criminal Law of Misdemeanor Domestic Violence, 1970-1990," *J Crim. L & Criminology*, 1992-1993, 83, 46.

12 Interstate Stalking, 18 USC, Section 2261A; Interstate Travel to Commit Domestic Violence, 18 USC, Section 2261; Interstate Violation of a Protection Order, 18 USC, Section 2262.

13 Full Faith and Credit, 18 USC, Section 2265, 2266; Full Faith and Credit for Child Support Orders Act,28 USC, Section 1738B; Civil Rights, 42 USC, Section 13981, 2000.

14 During the O.J. Simpson media frenzy in 1994-1996, more stories and feature stories on domestic violence issues appeared in print and electronic media venues than perhaps at any time in the last 40 years explaining the apparent reality

that Americans understood the importance of family violence issues during this period of time. This apparent awareness level faded in the consciousness of most Americans as media focus dissipated.

15 The battered women's movement had finally succeeded. The groundwork of the 1980s was reaping dividends. Susan Schecter said it well over 20 years ago, referring to the brief time between the mid-1970s and the early 1980s: "To start 500 shelters, win legal and social service reforms in hundreds of localities, form almost 50 state coalitions and capture the imagination of a nation in approximately eight years are extraordinary achievements. We owe a tremendous amount of gratitude to the founding leaders of the battered women's movement for their significant contributions."

16 See Robert Giles, *"Difficult Economic Times Prove Value of Multi-Disciplinary Approaches to Resolve Child Abuse,"* National Center for Prosecution of Child Abuse Update, Vol. 22 No. 1 (2009); Jerome Kolbo and Edith Strong, *"Multidisciplinary Team Approaches to the Investigation and Resolution of Child Abuse and Neglect: A National Survey",* 2 Child Maltreatment 1at 61 (1997).

17 The National Institute on the Prosecution of Domestic Violence was held February 23-26, 2010 in New Orlean, LA. It was sponsored by the Office on Violence Against Women, U.S. Department of Justice, Grant No. 2004-WT-AX-K047 and managed by Darla Sims, Program Manager. Darla Sims helped shape the program with Kristina Korobov, Training Coordinator, National District Attorneys Association.

18 Joan Kuriansky, *Promising Practices: Improving the Criminal Justice System's Response to Violence Against Women,* prepared by the STOP Violence Against Women Grants Technical Assistance Project, 1998, NCJ 172217. By 1998, the STOP TA Project had identified 19 national organizations with major roles related to domestic violence initiatives in America.

19 *Building an Effective Coordinated Community Response: Grants to Encourage Arrest Policies,* Conference Manual of the Battered Women's Justice Project, Washington, D.C., July 28-30, 1997.

   Family Violence—Building a Coordinated Community Response: A Guide to Communities, Chicago, IL, 1996; Barbara Hart, Barbara, *Coordinated Community Approaches to Domestic Violence,*(paper presented at the Violence Against Women Research Strategic Planning Workshop, National Institute of Justice, Washington, D.C., March 31, 1995.

20 K. Barnes et al., *Developing a Coordinated Community Response to Sexual Assault and Domestic Violence,* Ending Violence Against Women Project, Colorado, 1996.

21 *Model Protocol for Local Coordinating Councils on Domestic Violence,* Kentucky Governor's Council on Domestic Violence, 1997.

22 The new *Blueprint for Safety: An Interagency Response to Domestic Violence Crimes* (2010) in St. Paul, Minnesota is one of the best coordinated community response protocols in the country. The work of Ellen Pence, Jeff Edleson,

and a talented, multi-disciplinary team should be 'must reading' for domestic violence professionals across the United States and around the world. To obtain a copy of the blueprint, email blueprint@praxisinternational.org.

23 *Coordinating Community Responses to Domestic Violence,.* Melanie Shepard and Ellen Pence (eds.), Sage Publications. Thousand Oaks, CA, 1999. Ellen Pence has done an excellent job throughout her career of identifying the way system responses are generally developed to assist system professionals. Such protocols and policies are not generally designed with the victim's comfort and ease in accessing services as the primary goal.

24 The San Diego Story, and the local journey that laid the groundwork for the Family Justice Center is documented at www.familyjusticecenter.org under the "About Us" tab.

25 Presentation by Angela Fitzgerald, Director, Crime Victims Assistance Center, Shasta County District Attorney's Office, February 3, 2010, Redding, California.

26 See http://www.nyc.gov/html/ocdv/html/home/home.html. Accessed December 10, 2005. The New York City Family Justice Center (Brooklyn) is one of the 15 federally funded Family Justice Centers under the President's Family Justice Center Initiative funded by the U.S. Department of Justice, Office on Violence Against Women.

27 The Domestic Violence Enhanced Response Team (DVERT) in Colorado Springs, CO, began operating in 1997. DVERT was operated by the Colorado Springs Police Department and was nationally recognized for its successful collaborative approach—developing partnerships with 38 different public and private agencies. DVERT was one of the first co-located, multidisciplinary service approaches to domestic violence in the country. Intensive case management, crisis response, and a coordinated community response have been cited as the reason for successful outcomes in cases handled by DVERT.

CHAPTER THREE

Family Justice Centers

Sue Else was a college student at Iowa State University...when she started to think about the issues of violence against women. She saw what was happening to women, she saw the women's movement trying to respond. And she wanted to do something about it. She volunteered at Access, a domestic violence shelter in Ames, Iowa. She saw the pain of physically and sexually abused women. She saw their determination to overcome and it captured her. Sue would go on to work at and eventually lead the shelter. Later, she would have the opportunity to become CEO of Hope House with locations in Independence and Lee's Summit, Missouri. As she got deeper into the movement, she saw the need for her work and her agency to grow and evolve. She expanded services and reached out to other agencies. She saw the need for collaboration and helped found the Coordinated Community Councils to Prevent Domestic Violence in the cities of Independence, Lee's Summit, and Raytown, Missouri. She got grants to provide some services in-house with her own staff and added multiple programs. Her clients needed other services that Hope House could not provide so she led the effort to develop two campuses for the mission and work of Hope House, one in Independence and one in Lee's Summit. Her leadership led to the construction of two 52 bed shelters, two children's therapeutic centers, and two adult therapeutic centers. Her vision produced a safe visitation center, a civil legal program, and a part-

nership with a Hispanic domestic violence program. She started inviting other agencies to come serve her clients at Hope House—counselors, legal advisors, health care professionals. She built an alliance with the local police departments and they too started doing interviews and meeting with victims at Hope House instead of requiring them to go elsewhere. She did not want her clients to have to go from agency to agency and place to place. She had a deep understanding of where the domestic violence movement had come from but a strong commitment to how it must evolve and change over time—always staying accountable to survivors and listening to their needs and their challenges. Today, Sue is the President of the National Network to End Domestic Violence in Washington, D.C. She is still learning, still growing, still calling on the movement to keep evolving and changing. She also sits on the Advisory Board of the National Family Justice Center Alliance and provides that historical perspective to the movement toward greater co-located services on where we came from, and how we need to evolve as we keep seeking to provide better services to victims and their children. Sue has been honored with the National Family Justice Center Alliance's Lifetime Achievement Award and continues to be a powerful voice about the past…and the future of the family violence prevention movement in America and around the world.

Women like Sue Else and Ashley Walker pioneered the path for Family Justice Centers and other types of co-located service models. Ashley Walker, the founder of Battered Women's Services in San Diego, and I sat in a Denny's Restaurant in 1987 and talked about the idea of coordinating the services of the shelter, the City Attorney's Office, the Police Department, and other agencies beginning to work on issues surrounding family violence. We wrote our notes on a napkin. I was a new prosecutor assigned to handle domestic violence and she was a sexual assault survivor and passionate, fiery advocate for social justice and the rights of victims of violence and abuse. The very first written proposal for a comprehensive, multi-disciplinary, co-located service model grew out of that early meeting with Ashley Walker—advocate, shelter director, and powerful voice for survivors of sexual assault and domestic violence. We even listed our ideas in an order that would later be significant—Organize a task force, bring all the agencies together, recruit the support of elected officials, develop specialized units and programs, develop protocols, policies, and procedures, and co-locate all the services in one place!

Soon after meeting Ashley, former defense attorney Gael Strack joined the City Attorney's Office. She and I met in a courtroom. She was defending an abuser, I was the prosecutor. She was passionate, talented, and persuasive in front of a jury. After the case was over, I told her she should prosecute batterers instead of defending them! Months later, she was in the City Attorney's Office and joined our small little team of domestic violence prosecutors. And we kept adding allies to our numbers—Lt. Lesli Lord, DA Victim-Witness Coordinator Dee Fuller, family law attorney Lee Lawless, civil attorney Kate Yavenditti, survivor Deborah Feinstein, shelter advocate Denise Frey, YWCA advocate Elly Newman, sexual assault advocate Joyce Faidley, Gael, Ashley, myself, and a few others started meeting and dreaming.

At one of our earliest meetings, we decided we needed stationary. None of us had much power but we were sure that if we had stationary, we would seem far more important! So, creating stationary became a key step in changing the world! We talked much about the ideas of coordination, accountability, and co-location in those early days in 1988 and 1989.

It was not a new concept, co-locating services in one place, but it was already becoming clear to us and many others that the system was too hard for victims to navigate. Services were expanding. Agencies with programs for domestic violence victims were multiplying rapidly. It was good news in San Diego, and around the country, that proved we were beginning to realize the importance of dealing with violence. But the length of our referral list was already two pages—front and back!

Communities around the country were beginning to co-locate prosecutors and police officers to deal with domestic violence.[1] Some were bringing together staff from nonprofit, community-based organizations and law enforcement officials. The child advocacy movement had already proved that co-located services worked well. Battered women's shelters were expanding their multi-disciplinary services to meet needs beyond emergency shelter and food. But there were already far too many places for a victim to go if she needed help with many different needs as we discussed earlier in this book. So I wrote a proposal for our community with the help of Ashley Walker

AN IDEA WHOSE TIME HAD NOT COME

The original proposal for a Family Justice Center was about 10 pages long and was directed at the local District Attorney and City Attorney in San Diego. The proposal was simple: Bring together in one place, representatives from the District Attorney, City Attorney, Police Department, Sheriff's Department, the local battered women's shelter, and other social service providers. Then invite victims to come get help in one place. It was logical and just sheer common sense.

I was a young, new city prosecutor asking the elected County District Attorney to listen to me. Because my boss, the elected City Attorney, agreed to support my vision, the District Attorney gave me an audience with nearly 20 of his management staff. I passed out my proposal, made a 10-minute presentation, and sat down. There were no questions and discussion was limited. The next day I received a phone call from the Assistant District Attorney. The call was short, the message simple and direct. The DA did not support my proposal. My 1989 idea for all the services under one roof was an idea whose time had not come! Many of us were discouraged, but not deterred.

STARTING SMALL WITH THE VISION FOR CO-LOCATED SERVICES

Working with many of the advocates mentioned above from two local battered women's shelters, the San Diego Police Department, and other domestic violence prosecutors in the City Attorney's Office, Gael and I went forward with a portion of the concept anyway. With the blessing of then-San Diego City Attorney John Witt, we carved out three empty offices in the city prosecutor's office on the same floor as our specialized Domestic Violence Unit. We offered this space to the Police Department (to help us coordinate on the investigation and prosecution of cases), the YWCA Battered Women's Services (to offer support and advocacy to victims in our criminal cases), and the Center for Community Solutions (to operate a restraining order clinic). Their staff would do their own work with current caseloads in their current assignments while using the free office space. We offered this in return for only one promise: If we had victims on pending criminal cases who came to the City Attorney's Office, staff of the three invited agencies would sit down and talk to our victims and offer services as appropriate. It was a humble beginning.[2] And we kept adding allies. Sgt. Anne O'Dell joined us from the San Diego Police Department. She would go on to found the Domestic Violence Unit in the Police Department. Lt. Jim Barker would lead that Unit and join our collaborative efforts.

The co-location journey in San Diego was also aided by our creation first of the San Diego County Task Force on Domestic Violence and later by the creation of the San Diego Domestic Violence Council—coordinating councils that would help us recruit partner agencies, public officials, friends, and more allies.

As noted earlier, San Diego was not alone. Similar efforts were underway in Hennepin County, Minnesota; Mesa, Arizona; Phoenix, Arizona; Colorado Springs, Colorado; Albuquerque, New Mexico; and Indianapolis, Indiana. Sue Else and many other shelter directors were looking down the same road in shelters across America. Some multidisciplinary centers were based in hospitals, others in law enforcement agencies, others in battered women's shelters, courthouses, prosecutor's offices, and family advocacy programs on military bases. Depending on the strengths of a particular community, the approach might vary.

In communities with strong child advocacy centers, child advocacy programs began expanding their services to meet the needs of the adult victims of domestic violence while meeting the needs of abused children. The overarching goal of all similar programs was the same:

Provide more services to victims and their children from one location instead of expecting victims and their children to travel to many disparate agencies. The research supports our early vision, particularly with criminal justice system services included. A victim is more likely to use a system in the future knowing that the criminal justice system acted in a coordinated way in the past to support her.[3]

San Diego's journey continued during the 1990s without the support of the elected District Attorney. First, we co-located a few advocates with our prosecutors. Then we started rotating cops and prosecutors into each other's agencies a few days a week. In 1991, we added a partnership with Children's Hospital by supporting a new initiative developed by the Center for Child Protection, known as the Family Violence Project.[4] Slowly, we experienced firsthand the benefits of co-location, a multidisciplinary approach, and stronger day-to-day working relationships. Living together was so much more powerful than a community task force, a coordinating council, a phone list of resource agencies, or an e-mail distribution list. Living together as professionals was complicated, but it was evident early in our experience that it was providing the most efficient and effective services to victims we had ever delivered.

Finally, in 1998, we conducted our own version of a community safety audit as discussed briefly in the last chapter.[5] The idea was to evaluate how well we were doing in keeping battered women safe in our community. There were many aspects to the safety audit, but only one was necessary to prove the need for a Center. It was early in the audit that the following question arose: How many places does a victim of family violence have to go to get all the help she needs in our community? No one knew the answer. The answer would motivate us to begin the long journey toward changing the world.

After a day of brainstorming, charting, and evaluating we were finally able to answer the question — *in our community, in order for a victim to receive all necessary help she would have to go 32 different places!!* We discussed the issue of too many places to go in the last chapter but it is important to reiterate this realization. It is the heart of the need for co-located services. It is the heart of this book!

32 PLACES TO GO...WHAT NOW?

Results of the safety audit gave us our challenge. We knew our old idea's time had come; we resurrected that 1989 proposal. San Diego's Police Chief at the time, David Bejarano, was a community-oriented policing disciple. Dave Bejarano was part of San Diego's growing national reputation, built by former Chief (now Mayor) Jerry Sanders, as a department focused on problem-oriented policing. Indeed, by 1999, San Diego had officers doing tremendously innovative work with community organizations, using problem-oriented policing approaches to address chronic and entrenched problems.

By then, I had become the elected City Attorney. The City Attorney's Office developed a Neighborhood Prosecution Unit, which was supported by Chief Bejarano. The concept was simple. If it was effective to have police officers working in neighborhoods to address crime issues with community members, it would be even more helpful to have prosecutors assisting in the problem-solving process where the problems were actually occurring—in the neighborhoods.

Once the Neighborhood Prosecution Unit was created, the Chief and I sat down to talk about the community safety audit related to our domestic violence services. My proposal was straightforward: We needed to bring service providers together instead of requiring victims to go so many places for help. Though we did not know how many agencies might be willing to move portions of their staffs to such a location, we could certainly start with cops and prosecutors.

THE LOGICAL EXTENSION OF COMMUNITY POLICING

It took only one meeting for Chief Bejarano to figure it out. After I presented my proposal in 1998, he reflected on it briefly and then said these words: "This Center is the logical extension of our community policing and neighborhood prosecution work." Under the leadership of former Police Chief (now Mayor) Jerry Sanders, the San Diego Police Department had, as noted, become a national model for community-oriented policing. Chief Bejarano clearly saw the Family

Justice Center as the next step in the Department's community policing work. And the hard work began!

By late 1999, the Police Department had a specialized Domestic
Violence Unit with 24 detectives handling misdemeanor and felony
domestic violence cases, supervised by four sergeants and a lieutenant.
The City Attorney had a specialized misdemeanor prosecution unit
with a staff of 32, including 13 prosecutors, two investigators, three
advocates, and support staff. After all our work together, we could
lead the way. We would move in together, and we would invite social
service providers and other public agencies to join us in rent-free office space.

Critical mass toward the vision was gaining ground. Gael Strack
had become the President of the San Diego Domestic Violence
Council and challenged the Council to make the vision for the Family Justice Center their number one priority in 2002. They voted to
support the vision unanimously! Gael then developed a team with
Assistant Chief of Police Rulette Armstead, then-Sgt. Monica Kaiser, Lt. Jim Barker, Center for Community Solutions Director Verna
Griffin Tabor, Diane McGrogan, the head of the Social Services Program at Scripps Hospital, and others were recruited...relationship by
relationship...friend by friend...agency by agency...

The Chief's support was conditional upon a comprehensive study
of the feasibility of such a Center with a law enforcement presence.
He chose then-Sgt. Monica Kaiser to oversee the study. The study
took approximately 18 months, as Lt. Kaiser worked with Gael Strack
and pulled together a team that included prosecutors, police officers,
system advocates, and community-based advocates. They traveled
the country looking at other types of co-location models, including
child advocacy centers, sexual assault response teams, shelters, and
other small domestic violence programs with multidisciplinary services. They met with police officers, detectives, prosecutors, and local
community agency staff. They analyzed the potential case flow issues.
They evaluated the protocols necessary to protect chain-of-command
issues with the different agencies. The study's conclusion was clear:

The Family Justice Center idea could work with enough buy-in from policy makers, elected officials, and community agencies.

> It was an honor for me to be part of the original team that developed a model that was right for San Diego. Each community will need to figure it out for themselves and custom fit the Family Justice Center model to meet their needs, their strengths and weaknesses. But our journey has been worth the effort.
>
> Lt. Monica Kaiser, SDPD

Over the next six months, the study team of police officers, prosecutors, and community-based advocates led by Assistant Chief Rulette Armstead, Lt. Jim Barker, Sgt. Monica Kaiser, and Assistant City Attorney Gael Strack began figuring out what it would look like to have a few staff members from many different agencies move in together. There were myriad questions to be answered in planning for the actual operation of the Center:

- How much space would each agency get?

- Would the agency staff members be interspersed or segregated?

- Would all client services be provided on one floor or on multiple floors?

- How could the police officers be protected from supervision by prosecutors?

- How could the community agencies be assured that cops would not try to control them?

- What would the on-site governance structure look like?

- Who would be in charge?

- Who would be the final decision maker?

- Could a collaborative decision making model be used?

- How would non-governmental agencies have a say in day-to-day operations?

- How would clients enter the Center?

- Who would they see first?

- What records would be kept on clients?

- How would information on clients be shared between agencies?

NAME BASED ON SURVIVOR INPUT

During the evaluation process, the concept began to emerge under the working title of "San Diego Domestic Violence Service Center." With more discussion, the name evolved into "San Diego Domestic Violence Justice Center." However, after Lt. Kaiser's study gave the green light to the vision for the Center, our growing coalition and the entire Domestic Violence Council agreed it was time to float the idea with funding sources and, most importantly, with our potential clients—current victims and survivors of domestic violence in San Diego. So focus groups were developed and meetings were organized, as we reached out to talk to potential funders and clients. Gael Strack and others helped organize community forums and played a promotional video created by my press secretary, Maria Velasquez. We obtained a media sponsor to assist us in the outreach effort and the specific naming effort, the ABC affiliate, Channel 10.

Within a matter of weeks of reaching out to the community, the message came through loud and clear. Victims did not want to go to a *service center*. They did not want to go to a Center with the name *domestic violence*. Funding sources did not want to fund *domestic violence*. We considered and evaluated other names, and a clear consensus emerged: the San Diego Family Justice Center. Everyone supported *families*, and *justice* was critical in the process of stopping family violence. Justice would encompass both civil and criminal justice. Input from victims and survivors was also vital in concluding that offenders could not receive services at our Center. If we were going to create a safe environment for victims and their children, we must have a facility akin to a battered women's shelter, one where offenders were not welcome. The San Diego Family Justice Center would be solely a victim-centered facility, and victims would give support to one another.

> There's such a sense of security here. After experiencing what we go through you can become desensitized to the whole thing. Coming here provided me with a backbone. Here I was seeing other people who were here, all kinds of people, professional, from the street, people you would walk by everyday from all walks of life and have no idea they were going through the same thing that you were going through, too. It made me feel like I was not alone; other people have experienced what I went through, too. The people here who I talked with understood my situation and validated my experience. That made me stronger.
>
> Anonymous San Diego Family Justice Center Client, 2005

By October 2001, the concept was crystallized. The Center was viable. We had built a strong coalition. Nearly 20 years of raising awareness, collaboration, coordinated community response efforts, and specialization had produced a foundation for a Center with co-located services. But now how would we pay for it? The City of San Diego faced significant financial challenges. Social service programs already scrambled annually for scarce money. Where could we turn for support? Would the Mayor and Council appropriate general fund revenue for a new initiative like this? With so many competing priorities in local government, how could this one rise to the top of the list? We discuss resource issues and funding for the Center vision later in the book, but long before we figured out the larger business case, we had to fund our San Diego vision.

FINDING THE MONEY

Our first funding application went to the United States Department of Justice, Office on Violence Against Women (OVW) in 2001. We reasoned that this national idea should be endorsed at the federal level and San Diego should help lead the way. It made good sense, with so much federal money now focused on addressing family violence issues, that the Justice Department should support our exciting vision. But only months after applying for money, our application was rejected!

Though there were many reasons for our rejection, we received feedback from OVW that included two comments. First, we had asked for money to rent office space to create the Center, but at that time OVW provided funds only for program services. Second, our proposal had not fared well during the peer review process. OVW's peer review brought in domestic violence experts from across the country to evaluate all funding requests before staff made a final decision. Clearly, we failed in articulating our vision and/or the peer reviewers did not understand the concept of co-located services for victims of domestic violence and their children.

Though OVW rejected our first application, we had simultaneously submitted our application for rent and infrastructure costs to the California Endowment, a large private foundation focused on funding health-related initiatives in California. The Endowment carefully considered our proposal for many months. While our proposal was pending, we scheduled a public hearing in October 2001 before the City of San Diego's Public Safety and Neighborhood Services Committee. Made up of five members of the San Diego City Council, the committee was our first public presentation of the vision. We invited our Program Manager at the Endowment, Greg Hall, and other potential funders to the hearing.

We filled the committee hearing room with community supporters from a host of potential partner agencies. Momentum was building! Front and center was the Police Chief and the Fire Chief, in uniform, standing side by side with domestic violence advocates in support of a new public safety initiative in San Diego focused on helping victims of domestic violence. The committee heard the pitch, and they too saw the vision. They were moved as survivors shared their stories and the need for more accessible services. The hearing was not, however, about *those women* or *those victims*. We focused on the responsibility of our entire community to stop family violence. The committee voted to support the vision, though money still needed to be identified. Poignantly, two of the five members of the committee shared their own experiences with family violence, and both of them wrote a personal check to support the Center on the spot. The very

FJC On-Site and Off-Site Partners (2006 – 2010)

Action Network – Human Trafficking Coalition
Adult Protective Services
Cal Western Law School—Legal Internship Program
Camp HOPE
Center for Community Solutions—HOPE Team (Elder Abuse)
Children's Hospital—Chadwick Center, Family Violence Project
Dress for Success
FJC Legal Network
Military (Navy & Marine Corps)
San Diego City Attorney's Office—Child Abuse & Domestic Violence Unit
San Diego Deaf Mental Health Services
San Diego District Attorney's Office—Family Protection Division
Victim Assistance Program
San Diego Domestic Violence Council
San Diego County – Child Welfare Services
San Diego Family Justice Center Foundation
Family Justice Center Volunteer Program
San Diego FJC Chaplain's Program
San Diego Police Department—Domestic Violence Unit
San Diego Probation Department
San Diego Volunteer Lawyer Program – Family Law and Immigration Legal Services
San Diego State University (Stalking Assessment Project)
The Crime Victims Fund
Sharp Grossmont Hospital
Soul Care Project
Speak for Success – Women's Leadership Institute
UCSD - Forensic Medical Unit
Teen Court Juvenile Diversion Program
The Rainforest Art Project
Travelers Aid
Union Pan Asian Communities (UPAC)
Women, Infants and Children (WIC)
YWCA of San Diego County

first check was written by a City Council member, who in tears told me that he had seen his father hit his mother and he had not always acted "properly" with his wife.

Though new to the California Endowment, Greg Hall too saw the vision that day. Greg's insight and wisdom was the key turning point for the Center. Under the leadership of Dr. Robert Ross, the California Endowment became our gateway to success. Experienced in public health prevention and intervention models, Dr. Ross understood the concept of trying to bring all services together and developing a community of caring professionals who could focus on healing for victims. We also needed to identify potential City revenues to assist with the project. We did not want to take money away from existing programs. We wanted to make the pie bigger with new money from the General Fund of the City of San Diego. City Attorney analyst Mary Ann Stepnowsky became a secret weapon as she calculated the need and looked for potential funds to re-allocate from other city initiatives.

In March 2002, the California Endowment offered the City of San Diego a $500,000 challenge grant. If the City would match it, the Endowment would provide $500,000 over a three-year period to help make the Center a reality. Within 30 days, the Mayor and City Council pledged city community development block grant funds, and we had enough money to get started.

At every turn, we remembered the words of David Starr Jordan, the first President of Stanford University: "The world steps aside to let anyone pass who knows where they are going." We simply kept articulating where we were going until everyone around us came to believe it was true. We did not question that it would happen. We kept believing, stayed positive, and kept advocating to anyone that would listen. Once we had such diverse and strong support, we put the pressure on others to make sure they were not left off the list of supporters when the Center became a reality! And we kept circulating our support list to everyone—each time adding names of supporting agencies and supporting individuals. By the time we were done, we had over 70 agencies and individuals on the list. As we look back, we cannot remember an agency or individual that declined to be listed. Of course we were not asking for money yet…just their endorsement and support!

On April 9, 2002, then-Mayor Dick Murphy and a unanimous San Diego City Council authorized a five-year lease on privately owned downtown office space for the new Center. A local business-man, Chris McKellar, who had been touched by family violence in his own life, offered us three floors in a downtown high-rise at a reduced rent. And the space planning and detail work began in earnest.

Hope for Hurting Families II: How to Create a Family Justice Center in Your Community, available separately from this book, addresses the detailed steps necessary to open a Center.[6] A second edition of the manual, entitled *"Start Small: The Path to Creating a Family Justice Center in Your Community,"* will be published later this year. The first manual is based on the learning process we engaged in as we moved from concept to reality between October 2001 and October 2002, and is then supplemented with the lessons learned in communities across the United States between 2002 and 2007. The new manual will include the many lessons learned since 2007. Each of the manuals goes through the many steps we had to go through and also includes the unique dynamics we have now seen in more and more communi-ties that have gone down this road toward co-located services. But the overview in this chapter should give you a sense of the "COMPLI-CATED" part of figuring out a co-location model with 27 on-site and off-site partner agencies.

THE FAMILY JUSTICE CENTER—WHEN EVERYBODY WORKS TOGETHER

The first Family Justice Center in America officially opened on October 10. 2002. Over 170 people attended the grand opening cer-emony. San Diego did not invent co-located services, we just dreamed bigger than anybody had dreamed up until that day. In the first few months, we opened with seven agencies on site and served 100 cli-ents per month. I moved my entire Domestic Violence Unit from the City Attorney's Office into the Center (35 full-time staff including 13 prosecutors). The Police Chief moved in his entire Domestic Violence Unit (24 detectives and four sergeants). And two shelters joined us with advocacy staff, civil legal service providers joined us, and Sharp Grossmont Hospital sponsored our Forensic Medical Unit. Within two years, though many more agencies had come on board, and over 1,200 families were being served every month!

> Everyone was friendly, attentive, and comforting. No one judges you or makes you feel dumb or worthless. A lot of agencies have a talk-down mentality, but that attitude isn't here at the Family Justice Center. This is a great place and much needed. It would be nice to be given an envelope for legal papers so no one can see what I am carrying when I leave. When I go home, if he's there, I don't want him to see what I have."
>
> Lillian, Family Justice Center Client, 2004

Each week, nearly 120 professionals were providing services to victims and their children and were supported by a volunteer program that, at its peak, included more than 100 volunteers who attended a forty-hour training academy before joining the Family Justice Center team. Each volunteer committed a minimum of twelve hours per month for a year. The Center quickly gained national and international attention based on the qualitative feedback from clients participating in focus groups and exit interviews. Our first book documented many of those exit interviews and some have been included in this book.

The Center received multiple national awards from the U.S. Conference of Mayors, the National League of Cities, and others. It was also recognized for continuing the twenty-year decline in domestic violence homicides in the City of San Diego which gave San Diego the lowest domestic violence homicide rate of any major city in America.

Day in and day out in those early years of operation, under Gael Strack's leadership, there were "firsts" and "wows." We saw our first broken jaw in the Forensic Medical Unit in a woman only seeking a restraining order from the Center but unable to chew when we offered her food. We hosted our first baby shower for a client who was pregnant by her batterer but chose to keep the baby.

My daughter became the first Family Justice Center baby. The Family Justice Center gave me many resources so we could be safe from my abuser. My life has had many changes but, through the Family Justice Center and the great people that work there I can stand on my own two feet again. I'm a proud mother and have learned how not to be a victim.

Rachael Goodman, Former FJC Client

We were amazed to see how complex the needs were of many victims and how multiple services in the same place meant the world to them. We saw far less victims recanting their original statements to police when they were safe in the Center and everyone was working together to help them. We created an electronic filing process with the Family Court so that victims could apply for restraining orders and never have to go to court. We saw the power of providing counseling services for children in the same location where their mother was receiving her services.

We saw gay men and lesbian women come for help once we had gay and lesbian identified staff on site. We saw Pan-Asian victims once we had Union of Pan Asian Communities on site providing services. We saw Latino clients once we had bi-lingual services. We saw deaf

It is well documented that disabled people are victimized at twice the rate of others. There are an estimated 350,000 deaf and hard of hearing people in San Diego County. They are often invisible and are a critically underserved population. Being able to bring domestic violence services to our clients, with the help of all the Family Justice Center partners has provided a level of accessibility that this community has never had before. The impact is immeasurable. We are grateful for the smiles we get when our clients realize there are deaf professionals on site to help them. We are truly changing the meaning of accessibility for all at the Family Justice Center.

Allison Sepulveda, Executive Director
National Center for Deaf Advocacy

women coming forward for the first time once we brought the National Center for Deaf Advocacy in as an on-site partner.

A CHRISTMAS STORY

Two years after the Center was fully operational, we saw in vivid living color…through the lived experience of a real, flesh and blood victim what the FJC (hitting on all cylinders) could do in the life of someone in need.

It was the holiday season and Gael had just been named the official Director of the Center after two years of an informal leadership structure in which she led the Center as an Assistant City Attorney. She left City Hall intent on enjoying a two-hour shopping spree at Horton Plaza, the city's downtown shopping mall. But her attention was drawn to a young woman with a suitcase at her side sitting in the lobby of City Hall. Her head was buried in her hands; a small child tugged at her side. Gael could not walk by. She stopped and asked the young woman if she was okay. The woman looked up and began crying.

The young woman had just been beaten. Her injuries were obvious. Fleeing her boyfriend, she had ridden the city's mass transit trolley system to downtown San Diego. She did not know where to go or what to do. She had so many concerns and needed help with so many different things. Gael never got to the shopping mall that day. Within 30 minutes, she escorted Renee to the nearby San Diego Family Justice Center. Kimberly Pearce, the Director of Client Services, welcomed her. A dedicated volunteer took the traumatized child, changed her diaper, provided a snack, and engaged the child with toys on the floor of the children's room. Kimberly informed Renee of the options available to her and developed a plan of action. A forensic nurse conducted a medical exam and documented Renee's injuries.

Next, Renee took a hot shower in the Forensic Medical Unit and received a clean set of clothes. A San Diego police officer took a courtesy report, though Renee lived outside of the city limits. She was afraid to call her dad. Instead, she chose to meet with Chaplain

George Barnes and receive some spiritual support. At Renee's request, Chaplain George called her dad for her and talked him through the unfolding drama. A social worker from Traveler's Aid assisted in making arrangements for Renee to travel to the Midwest the next morning to stay with her parents.

Shortly thereafter, Renee met with a shelter representative and received authorization for emergency shelter. We ultimately purchased her bus ticket and provided her $20 in spending money. Chaplain George transported her to the nearby shelter that night. The next morning, Chaplain George, who Renee had connected with on a very meaningful level, brought her to the Center for follow-up services.

Renee asked to meet with Gael before she left. She said she had no idea that such a place existed. Gael told her of the Center's recent beginning and reflected with Renee that if they had met just two years earlier in that City Hall lobby, Gael's only recourse would have been to refer her to the series of places she needed to go for help. Gael and Renee had both experienced the power of the Family Justice Center, and Renee and her little girl's life would never be the same. Later in the morning, George Barnes drove her and her daughter to the bus station and waited until her bus departed for home, where her parents were waiting for her. Co-located services, all talking, all working together, all in one place…magic.

Three other key events are important to discuss here to document the history of the co-located services movement and the journey from the San Diego Family Justice Center to centers now developing around the United States and around the world. Again, knowing where we have come from will help us see where we are going. And it will help to understand why the many Centers we discuss in the rest of this book are now in existence.

OPRAH WINFREY SAYS "WHO'S GONNA DO THAT? 32 DIFFERENT AGENCIES!"

In 2003, soon after opening the San Diego Family Justice Center, I was invited to be on the Oprah Winfrey Show. Oprah profiled and praised the Family Justice Center model. Her profile of the Center is still available on her website and on the National Family Justice Center Alliance website. Her famous line was delivered right near the beginning of her discussion of the Center and interview of me: "Some people who work in the domestic violence field admit that if they were victims of domestic violence themselves they would not choose to report it or choose to go through the system…after finding out what a victim would have to go to, 32 different agencies to get help, the City of San Diego launched a new solution…because who's gonna do that? 32 different agencies!"[7]

Oprah Winfrey helped launch the Family Justice Center vision and promote the entire movement toward co-located services for victims and their children. Her show is syndicated around the world. Within a year of appearing on Oprah, we had site visitors from over 70 countries come and visit the Center. We had visitors from nearly all fifty states. She played a powerful role in helping us spread the word about our own success and in promoting the simple idea of having services in one place.

PRESIDENT GEORGE W. BUSH—"THE RUNAROUND IS OVER IN SAN DIEGO."

The second major development in the first two years of the exciting start up of the San Diego Family Justice Center was the decision by the President of the United States to profile San Diego and offer money to communities to figure out what co-location would look like in their community.

In April 2003, I attended a White House Roundtable on Family Violence organized by Lifetime Television. I participated in a panel at the White House with Attorney General John Ashcroft, Secretary of Health and Human Services Tommy Thompson, Office on Violence Against Women Director Diane Stuart, Domestic Policy Advisor to the President Margaret Spellings, singer Michael Bolton, National Network to End Domestic Violence President Lynn Rosenthal, and others to discuss the future of the national movement to stop family violence. During the meeting, we were each given five minutes to give our views on the future of the domestic violence movement and what the President should do to help move it forward. I advocated for two major ideas: that the President should speak in a national address on the issue of family violence; and that the administration should support innovative, forward-looking initiatives such as the San Diego Family Justice Center. I argued that without new approaches to service delivery, the national domestic violence movement would continue to proliferate services to victims without providing the most efficient, easily accessible services.

Six months later, Gael Strack and I were invited to participate in a White House event on October 8, 2003 hosted by the President to recognize Domestic Violence Awareness Month. Prior to the event, I met privately with the President and Diane Stuart, the Director of the Justice Department's Office on Violence Against Women ("OVW") and then joined over 150 national leaders in the domestic violence movement for a presidential address. In his October 8th speech, President Bush said "The runaround is over in San Diego" and announced the President's Family Justice Center Initiative designed to create Family Justice Centers across America modeled after the San Diego Family Justice Center.[8] Subsequently, Diane Stuart from the OVW was asked to take the lead on this pilot program to develop fifteen similar centers in communities across the country.

By January 2004, over 400 communities responded with letters of intent to the United States Department of Justice's announcement of the Family Justice Center Initiative, and our team in San Diego was asked to serve as the comprehensive technical assistance provider for the entire initiative. On July 21, 2004, Attorney General Ashcroft announced that the Department of Justice was awarding more than $20 million to fifteen communities chosen under President Bush's Family Justice Center Initiative to prevent and respond to violence against women.[9] Furthermore, five communities would receive technical assistance grants to provide specialized expertise and consultation. The fifteen recipients of the Initiative awards were selected, among other criteria, based on geographic distribution, economic and cultural diversity, service to underserved populations, and coordination with Native American communities.[10]

CONGRESS ADDS FAMILY JUSTICE CENTERS TO THE VIOLENCE AGAINST WOMEN ACT IN 2005

In 2005, the Congress of the United States recognized the importance of co-located services in the domestic violence movement and the success of the Family Justice Center model in many communities by denoting Family Justice Centers and other types of co-located, multi-agency service delivery models as a "purpose area" in Title I of the Act.[11] This significant and historic federal legislation has allowed many more communities to seek federal assistance in planning and operating Family Justice Centers and other co-located service models. Preliminary outcomes documented by the U.S. Department of Justice and individual Centers have included reduced domestic violence homicides, increased victim safety, increased autonomy, increased empowerment for victims and professionals, reduced fear and anxiety for victims and their children with the court system, increased peer support, reduced witness recanting, and increased numbers of victims receiving services.[12]

CORE SERVICES IN FAMILY JUSTICE CENTERS

As the movement toward co-located services has evolved it has become clear that each community is unique, the mix of services will

The day I came to the center I was afraid. I had lost all hope. My advocate helped me understand and helped me see the strengths that I have. The one thing that I learned was that no one can take my strengths away. Taking the first step was the hardest but the most important one in my life. While I sat through the assessment all that I could think was that this was my last stop. Walking in I was not sure what to expect but to have someone listen to me and help guide me through all the services made the difference. Through the 13 years that I lived with abuse, I always felt as if no one was listening, as if no one cared what I was going through. When I came here I realized that there are people here that understood and were willing to help me. I now feel that I can move forward with confidence.

Maria, Anaheim Family Justice Center Client
(Anaheim, CA), 2010

vary by community, models of co-location will differ depending on the needs of victims in a community, and the interaction among partner agencies will depend on the strength of the collaborative relationships among all participating partners. The number one service requested by clients in most Family Justice Centers in America is civil legal services followed closely by counseling and safety planning. This was true soon after we opened the San Diego Family Justice Center and we have seen similar results in Centers across the United States. The primary civil legal service is a domestic violence restraining order. And in many Centers, the goal is to let a client apply for a restraining order without having to go to court (electronic filing). Centers in Anaheim, California; Tulsa, Oklahoma; and New York City, New York and other communities are now using video teleconferencing with the courts to produce an even better communication platform between the Family Justice Center and the court system. Court is a scary place for domestic violence victims and they would much rather come to a Family Justice Center, put their children in free child care, and then work with an advocate and a lawyer to seek the needed legal protection. In our "how to" manuals we talk far more about how to set up such processes, but it should be called out here that a victim's legal needs relating to legal protection, child custody, child support, and divorce (if necessary) are the most pressing needs for most victims when they come asking for help.

The primary services in most Family Justice Centers include:

- Food

- Clothing

- Restraining orders (without going to court)

- Free cell phones with free minutes (Thanks to Verizon's Hope Line Program)

- Free Internet access

- Spiritual support

- Transportation assistance

- Free medical and dental assistance

- DA Victim-Witness Assistance services

- Counseling

- Support groups

- Safety planning

- Child care

- Support services for children

- Law enforcement assistance (police and prosecutors)

- Free locksmith services

- Pregnancy counseling

And all the services are in one place! They are real and tangible.

> I walked in with the impression that it was a small court facility for Injunctions and to my amazement I walked into a safe, caring, patient, and resourceful as well as informative staff and center with many services. Thank you so much!
>
> Nancy, Hillsborough County Family Justice Center Client (Tampa, FL) - 2009

And, as the movement is evolving, many Centers are adding much more sophisticated services for victims and their children:

- Economic/financial assessments

- Financial/literacy/credit counseling

- Credit repair

- Asset development

- Educational classes

- Personal coaching

- Mentoring opportunities for all clients (adults and children)

- Job training

- On-site housing—emergency, transitional, and affordable

- On-site job availability for victims and children through corporate partnerships with responsible retailers

- Coffee shop for clients (E.g. Bosco's Café in the Alameda County FJC)

Client complaints, though a very small percentage of feedback received in most Centers, help us focus on services they still want us to add in Centers and on the waiting time when there are many clients going through the intake process at the same time.

> I thought I was coming to a business to fight my way through horrible experiences. I want to say thank you for reminding me there are kind people in this world that help you and have hope and energy when you think you have none. All of them together gave me what I needed to deal with it all!
>
> Maria, Crystal Judson Family Justice Center Client
> (Tacoma, WA) - 2009

Centers solicit complaints and try to respond to them if at all possible. But even beyond the amazing array of services now being provided from a single location, Centers have also adopted the National Family Justice Center Alliance vision statement that points the way into the future and can point the way for communities across America.

FAMILY JUSTICE CENTER MOVEMENT VISION STATEMENT

A future where ALL the needs of victims are met, where children are protected, where violence fades, where economic justice increases, where families heal and thrive, where hope is realized, and where we ALL work together…

The vision is big and sometimes hard to make tangible. The motto we have adopted to keep us moving forward keeps it simple and is the

The Alameda County Family Justice Center grew from an idea to one of the most amazing journeys I have ever witnessed. We dreamed big enough that we were able to bring together over 20 agencies with staff in one place. The County provided a vacant building and provided incredible support in making the building exactly the way the clients told us it would work for them. The local non-profit agencies identified key staff members that should be there. Then, we moved in the prosecutors, the police officers, the victim-witness advocates, and the other county employees that provided services to victims. Today, we are a successfully thriving Center serving well over 200 new families per month. The big dream has changed the world for us in Alameda County.

Nancy O'Malley
Alameda County District Attorney

title of this book: DREAM BIG! Daily, the dedicated professionals at many of the Centers challenge each other to dream big and keep listening to clients as they tell us what is working and what is not. Clients each dream of lives free from violence and abuse. The least we can do is dream with them as we continue to build partnerships with more and more agencies that can wrap their arms around our clients whenever necessary.

The bigger you dream, the more you can do to give hope to those in need. In the beginning, for example, I never would have imagined that we would make spiritual support a priority in Family Justice Centers with cops and prosecutors present, but we listened to our clients, looked at the research, and dreamed big! Today, chaplains (ordained clergy and trained lay people) participate in nonsectarian, interfaith programs in many Centers and provide powerful encouragement to clients suffering from trauma and in shock.

The power of dreaming big produced tremendous encouragement to staff and clients through the dedicated service of a host of volunteer chaplains!

Is there more to be done? Yes. We don't have enough services to help victims get job training and jobs. We don't have enough legal services. We need to do more to provide affordable, long-term housing for clients. We have a long way to go, but the Center vision is moving us forward one step at a time!

Attending to clients' legal, emotional, and physical needs is the first priority but their spiritual needs are just as important. In my years working at the Family Justice Center, I continue to see amazing results by having Chaplaincy services available to clients at the very place where they are receiving their other services. If a chaplain were not there at that crucial place and time, it is most likely clients would not open up about their faith crisis and would not find a person capable to discuss spirituality and domestic violence.

Knoxville Family Justice Center Chaplain Dr. David Kitts

CONCLUSION

San Diego did not invent co-location. San Diego just dreamed bigger than anyone had dreamed before when we brought together staff from 27 agencies in one place and let victims choose what services they wanted and needed. But thanks to Oprah, the President of the United States, the Congress of the United States, and now many other visionaries and dreamers in communities across the United States and around the world, the effort toward co-located service models has accelerated.

Communities now have diverse models. Centers in New York City (NY), Duluth (MN), Tampa (FL), New Orleans (LA), Monroe (LA), Tulsa (OK), Knoxville (TN), Buffalo (NY), Salt Lake City (UT), San Antonio (TX), Albuquerque (NM), Rockville (MD), Peoria (IL), Nampa (ID), Tacoma (WA), Anaheim (CA), Oakland (CA), Tampa (FL), Montgomery (AL), and many other cities and counties are helping us figure it out. It has been a long journey. It has been years and years of relationship building. It has been strong, decisive decision making at key moments in time that said, "We must do this though the unknowns far outnumber the knowns."

This new service delivery model can be done and is a promising approach to dealing with the current services for victims of family violence and their children in many communities that require victims to go from place to place, agency to agency, telling their story over and over again. The survivors battling through your current systems just need you to keep reading…and then do something about it.

NOTES

1   A host of communities developed some version of co-located domestic violence services during the 1990s that included a number of law enforcement professionals, including Santa Clara County, CA; Seattle, WA; Colorado Springs, CO; Newport News, VA; Nashville, TN; Memphis, TN; Chattanooga, TN; San Jose, CA; Quincy, MA; Hennepin County, MM; Phoenix, AZ; Mesa, AZ; and Indianapolis, IN.

2   See more elements of our journey in *The San Diego Story* at www.familyjustice-center.org.

3   E. Gondolf and E. Fisher, *Battered Women as Survivors: An Alternative to Treating Learned Helplessness,* Lexington: D.C. Heath & Co. 1988

4   The Family Violence Program was developed by Sandy Miller, M.S., after she was hired by the Center for Child Protection at Children's Hospital in 1989 to assist in reducing foster care placements within the child protective system. Sandy was a domestic violence-trained advocate who developed a specialized advocacy unit with trained domestic violence advocates assigned to work with battered women where there was a co-occurrence of child abuse and domestic violence.

5   Ellen Pence and her team in Duluth, MN, have developed the concept of a community safety audit, a process by which a community evaluates its systems and intervention responses. Though Ellen has had a strong partnership with San Diego, she did not participate personally in our 1998 assessment process. We did, however, use the assistance of a number of consultants who had received training in Duluth on the community safety audit process.

6   *Hope for Hurting Families II: How to Start A Family Justice Center in Your Community* (2008) is available on-line at www.familyjusticecenter.org.

7   Oprah Winfrey Show, January 2003.

8   Press Release, The White House, President Bush Proclaims October Domestic Violence Awareness Month (Oct. 8, 2003), *available at* http://www.whitehouse. gov/news/releases/2003/10/20031008-5html; Joe Hughes, *San Diego's Family Justice Center is Hailed by Bush*, SAN DIEGO UNION-TRIBUNE , Oct. 9, 2003, *available at* http://www.signonsandiego.com/news/metro/20031009-9999_1m9center.html.

9   Press Release, Dep't of Justice, Justice Department to Spearhead President's Family Justice Center Initiative to Better Serve Domestic Violence Victims (Oct. 8, 2003), *available at* http://www.usdoj.gov/opa/pr/2003/October/03_ojp_560.htm.

10 The fifteen communities receiving the awards were: County of Alameda, Oakland, California; Bexar County, San Antonio, Texas; City of Boston, Boston, Massachusetts; Defiance Municipal Court, Defiance, Ohio; County of Erie, Buffalo, New York; Hillsborough County, Tampa, Florida; City of Knoxville, Knoxville, Tennessee; City of Nampa, Nampa, Idaho; City of New York, Brooklyn, New York; Ouachita Parish Police Jury, Monroe, Louisiana; Sitka

Tribe of Alaska, Sitka, Alaska; Somos Familia Family Institute, Inc., Las Vegas, New Mexico; St. Joseph County, South Bend, Indiana; City of St. Louis, St. Louis, Missouri; City of Tulsa, Tulsa, Oklahoma. *See id.*

11 OFFICE OF VIOLENCE AGAINST WOMEN, THE PRESIDENT'S FAMILY JUSTICE CENTER INITIATIVE BEST PRACTICES 2–4 (2007), *available at:* http://www.usdoj.gov/ovw/docs/pfjci_bestpractices_overview2007.pdf.

12 Id.

Caution: Not All Communities
Are Ready (Or Willing)

Casey Gwinn and Gael Strack

Judge Ron Adrine has been working the field of family violence for nearly 30 years. He served as a prosecutor in the Cuyahoga County Prosecutor's Office early in his career, worked for the House Select Committee on Assassinations, and in private practice with his dad. He became a judge in 1981 and helped create and manage the Cleveland Municipal Court's Domestic Violence Case Calendar. He is politically connected, zealous, driven, and passionate about stopping family violence. When he first heard about the Family Justice Center opening in San Diego in 2002, he wanted one in Cleveland more than almost anything he had ever aspired to create in the domestic violence prevention world. He brought Gael Strack to Cleveland in 2003 to share the vision with everyone that would listen. And she started the dreaming in Cleveland! But Judge Adrine knew that the time was not right. He helped Cleveland investigate applying for the President's Family Justice Center Initiative in 2004. But there were too many disagreements, too many conflicts among agencies, and too many issues to be resolved regarding coordination. After the movement began to expand, he looked at it again in 2005, 2006, 2007, and 2008. But he needed the right team, he needed buy-in, and he needed supporters to realize that co-located services were critical to reducing Cleveland's high domestic violence homicide rate. Cleveland was not ready until 2009 when Judge Adrine's team obtained grant funds and began the process of planning for a Family Justice Center. Wisely, they planned for a two year journey. There are many good people in Cleveland but the more good people and programs the tougher it would be to get everyone together. Finally, Cleveland was ready to roll up their sleeves, start the dialogue, and bring the agencies together. Over 50 agencies and nearly 100 people met in August 2009. The first day there was healthy dialogue but still a great deal of discussion about whether Cleveland even needed such a Center. But the morning of the second day, it became clear that Ron Adrine's vision was the right one and it was time. Crystal Waters was murdered in Cleveland during the planning meetings for the Cuyahoga Family Justice Center. Her body was dumped in a dumpster. A number of the agencies represented at the meeting had dealt with Crystal but there was little communication, no coordination, and no successful intervention with Crystal and her boyfriend. Now, Crystal was dead and everyone knew it was time. Cleveland was ready to start a working together in earnest on a co-located services model.

While some communities may find that a Center is not suited for their particular circumstances, more commonly others find they are simply not yet ready to pursue the Family Justice Center vision. The Center vision can be articulated by one or many in a community but it should only become a reality through an organic process. The vision cannot and should not be imposed from the outside or from the top down. It must grow from the bottom up. It is based on relationships between individuals and agencies. Those relationships must evolve over time and develop to a point where moving in together is a healthy idea. Sometimes different elected officials or policy makers are needed to advance the vision as well because entrenched leaders and bureaucratic agencies don't want to change and don't want to work hard enough to re-orient their agencies and their systems toward a coordinated community response model or a co-located services model.

In other communities we find that professionals don't want to change the way they do business. They have systems set up for their own convenience and they are so used to the way they do business they don't want to change how they do business. In this chapter even as we put out the caution that not all communities are ready, you will see testimonials from professionals that have worked in Centers to make the point about how powerful the model is for those that are willing to change their approach. You will not see text boxes from survivors here praising the co-located services model as you do in other chapters but you will see the ringing endorsements of many professionals from San Diego and elsewhere. They are meant to be a challenge to those that say they don't need a Center or they don't support the model.

Just like people, agencies that don't trust each other and don't know how to work together should not live together. Let's look more closely at each idea being developed here: 1) The Center vision must grow out of a long, organic process of collaboration and specialization within a local community; 2) Communities should assess whether they have the building blocks for development of an effective Center. *If communities are not ready, they should not pursue this vision*; and 3) Some agencies, public and private, are unwilling to do the hard work that is necessary to move toward a co-located services model

RESPECTING AND UNDERSTANDING THE RELATIONSHIP—BUILDING JOURNEY

No community can wake up one day and decide to build a Center. It has to grow into the idea over time. The cops and prosecutors need to have learned how to investigate and prosecute batterers successfully. The shelter advocates need to have developed close working relationships with those cops and prosecutors. Bringing everyone to a meeting, putting name tags on them, and then telling them they are now going to live together 16 hours a day in a Family Justice Center is not a good idea.

San Diego's relationship-building journey toward a Center began over 20 years ago.[1] It had its roots in the decision of feminist ad-

Being at the Family Justice Center has been a very humbling experience.
I now realize how many victims are depending on us to get this right and
that the case does not end with a conviction. The healing process is much
bigger than just one system's response. Victims need all of us—medical,
legal, and social agencies—to work together. And when we do, you can
literally see the difference. They reclaim their inner strength and beauty so
much faster.

Gael Strack, CEO, National Family Justice Center Alliance
Founding Director
San Diego Family Justice Center

vocates to build relationships with criminal and civil justice professionals. It grew because of the decision of feminists in San Diego
to include men. Former YWCA Battered Women's Services Director
Ashley Walker recently recounted the intentional choice to reach out
to men in the early and mid-1980s, seeking alliances instead of en-
gendering conflict.[2]

San Diego never had a class action lawsuit against law enforcement agencies for failing to protect battered women. Little animosity
ever developed there between battered women's shelters and criminal justice professionals. The cooperative spirit was aided by a core
group of key system professionals who allied themselves with feminist
advocates from 1986 to 1988.[3] As a result, there was a relationship
of collegiality and camaraderie from our earliest task force planning
meetings. At times there was finger pointing and blaming, but we
made a conscious effort to realize it and stop it whenever it started.

In many communities, the nature of the relationship between
shelter advocates and criminal and civil justice professionals will be
the key dynamic that determines whether a Center can evolve and
flourish. Communities where, for a variety of reasons, conflict and
mistrust exist between shelter advocates and law enforcement professionals are likely to find it difficult to build a collaborative approach
that can lead to co-location of services.

We have a number of Family Justice Centers in major cities in
America today where the relationship between the criminal justice
system and the shelter was strained before they started planning a

Family Justice Center and starting a Center only made it worse. It always makes us sad to see that. Family Justice Centers can operate with many partners and have a very positive impact on the lives of battered women and their children but it is always so much stronger if the local shelter is involved from the beginning and stays involved.

KEY STEPS IN THE FAMILY JUSTICE CENTER JOURNEY

Key steps in communities that have successfully pursued Family Justice Centers before even beginning to plan for a Center may help other communities trying to pursue this vision, including the following:

- Established and operated a domestic violence task force or coordinating council

- Created specialized Domestic Violence Units in the DA's Office, City Attorney's Office, Probation Department, and Police Department

- Developed and maintained strong relationships between police, prosecutors, and community-based shelter/domestic violence agencies and programs

- Held community forums and victim focus groups confirming the need for a Center

- Obtained support from the Mayor/City Council or the County Commissioners/Board of Supervisors including some level of a funding commitment

- Maintained a close working relationship with the statewide domestic violence coalition.[4]

At every turn, communities that have been successful have progressed, sometimes slowly, toward the ultimate vision of a Center. Key steps that have been identified in the development of a strong coordinated community response are usually present if a Family Justice Center is going to be viable in a community.[5] Many authors have also identified the importance of community leaders dedicated to advancing social reforms in the domestic violence field.[6] Most successful communities have had strong leadership from key policy makers, including agency heads and elected officials. In New York City, Mayor Bloomberg has led the way with very strong leadership from Yolanda Jimenez, the Commissioner of the Office to Combat Domestic Violence. In Alameda County, District Attorney Nancy O'Malley was the visionary and leader from the beginning. She had the key relationships with policy makers, business leaders, and community leaders as the planning process moved forward. She also had the credibility of working in the sexual assault and domestic violence community for more than 20 years. In New Orleans, Mary Claire Landry, the Director of Crescent House, was central to their success. She led the largest shelter, she had a high public profile in the community, and she had the respect of government leaders, faith community leaders, and people working in the trenches of the movement. Indeed, in any community with strong success in collaborative, co-located, multi-agency services, we can identify a leader or leaders that have paved the way and kept the community on track as it has moved forward toward the vision.

KEY ELEMENTS OF A COMMUNITY READY FOR A FAMILY JUSTICE CENTER

In the last ten years, diverse communities—tribal, rural, suburban, and urban—considering a Center vision have found over and over that key elements must be in place for successful development of a Center. Anyone in a community advocating for creation of such a Center needs to know what pieces must be in place for those agencies and people to make it a reality.

- Critical partners necessary to a Center planning process include police and prosecution professionals, shelter and community-based advocates, civil legal services providers, medical professionals, and diverse community-based organizations. All must be willing to first study the practical implications of moving in together;

- Criminal justice agencies should have a history of developing aggressive arrest, investigation, and prosecution policies that keep victims safe while the system prosecutes the batterer. *Criminal justice agencies with dangerous or irresponsible policies or practices that condone high mutual arrest rates or allow the re-victimization of victims by officers or system professionals, are not ideal candidates for co-located services with community-based shelter organizations;*

- Potential Center partnering agencies must be willing to accept the victim-centered service delivery model of the vision and reject on-site services for batterers. The vision is to provide **on-site services to victims and their children only** in order to avoid the increased danger and intimidation that comes from batterers being allowed access to them when victims come forward for help;

- The core community partners—police, prosecutors, and community-based advocates— should have a history of specialization in their domestic violence intervention work—specially trained advocates, police officers, prosecutors, judges, court support personnel, and medical professionals who focus most, if not all, of their time and energy on handling domestic violence cases;

- Local elected officials and government policy makers must engage early in discussions about the development of a Center and pledge their public support.

Quite a list, isn't it? Just when this book started to get you excited about the Center vision, you see a checklist that makes creating the right foundation a very tall order indeed. But the basics should be clear. This list was not made up out of the blue. It was forged in the experience of "pouring the footings" for many of the first Centers in the United States, Canada, and Great Britain and then confirmed over and over again as Centers have developed across the United States, Canada, Great Britain, Mexico, Jordan, and Australia. Creat-

> The Family Justice Center concept offers the best approach to bringing together not only agencies helping domestic violence victims but bringing together services for elder abuse, child abuse, and sexual assault victims as well. We cannot continue to do business in this country in separate movements. We must become one movement, with everyone working well together and completely focused on meeting the needs of victims instead of meeting the needs of the system.
>
> Bonnie M. Dumanis, San Diego County District Attorney

ing a Family Justice Center is not so easy. The Family Justice Center is a very simple idea that is very hard to turn into reality. And even after turning it into reality, it is very hard to keep a Center healthy, dynamic, and vibrant over time.

We will discuss the importance of leadership and the challenges in Family Justice Centers in a couple later chapters, but the problems that crop up often have their roots in issues that were not properly addressed and solved even before a Center opens. It is why conducting a community assessment at the beginning is so critical.

> The synergy of community partners, law enforcement, prosecutors, and civil attorneys all working together creates a novel and formidable force to be reckoned with.
>
> Steve Allen, Civil Attorney

ASSESSMENT QUESTIONS FOR ANY COMMUNITY

In some cases, asking questions may be a better way to get at the issues discussed previously. We have identified a series of 10 questions to be applied by potential funders of a Center proposal.

Any community that is considering developing a Center should answer the following questions itself in an honest, open, objective community conversation. Community members advocating for creation of a Center can ask their elected officials to hold public meetings and discuss these questions. They are an excellent starting point for discussing whether your community has the right background, history, and committed partners to make a Center work.

1. Do you have protocols for every agency in your community on how it responds to domestic violence? When were the protocols last updated?

2. Does the state domestic violence coalition work closely with your community or strongly support your existing protocols and procedures?

3. Do you have a history of agencies working together? Do you respect each other?

4. Do you have domestic violence specialists in your law enforcement agencies and in your prosecutor's office?

5. Do you have a domestic violence task force or coordinating council?

6. What is the greatest accomplishment of that task force in the last year?

7. Who will be your strongest partner in pursuing the Center vision?

8. Who will be your weakest partner in pursuing the vision?

9. How much local money is already being spent in your community to help victims of domestic violence? Has the amount of money gone up or down over the last 10 years?

10. What will you do to pursue the Center vision if you cannot initially find funding?[7]

11. How many places does a victim have to go to get help in your community?

RECOGNIZING THE TRUTH—EVEN IF IT HURTS

No community wants to conclude it is not ready for the exciting vision of a Center model. Sharon Denaro from Dade County, Florida, agreed that the readiness issue is huge for any community:

Once we got into figuring out how to develop a Center and run it, I had a new appreciation for strategic planning. It can be extremely painful but absolutely necessary to ask the right questions and then figure out the right model for a community. It is the key to success. Once we were operational, we went to trial less. Trials dropped by more than 50%. Less victims re-canted. More defendants pled guilty. When you have a Forensic Medical Unit working with detectives, cases don't go to trial.

Deputy District Attorney Tim Campen

When the President's Family Justice Center solicitation came out [in 2004], we wanted to apply. We had a core group of individuals who wanted to see it happen and we had a wonderful history of working together especially in developing a domestic violence court. However, we also discovered we were not ready. The idea of a Family Justice Center was new and it had not been discussed with everyone. We needed to get buy-in from key government officials, our advocacy community and a Champion needed to emerge. The good news is the solicitation gave us an opportunity to begin the discussion. We now have some great discussions going on and the pieces are falling into place. We've been energized by the Family Justice Center concept. We have hope that we can make a difference in Dade County with this vision but we are not ready yet.[8]

As this book continues, the powerful success of the Family Justice Center vision will become more and more evident. Any community leader or agent for change will catch the excitement and want to be part of it. But it does a great disservice to the complexity of this vision and to the unique nature of different communities if we pretend the vision is right for every community everywhere at any time. But if it is not the Family Justice Center, you need to find other steps to take to move closer to what a Center can accomplish.

OKAY TO NOT BE READY

The message here is to relax—slow down! Don't try to force-feed this vision to anyone. Every community needs visionaries and advocates for creation of a Center. But it takes time for everyone to see the vision and be ready to pursue it. We need to continually acknowledge the following:

> What would normally take us a week to get accomplished only takes us a day in a Family Justice Center. We can also assist multiple clients without ever having to leave the Center—one client may be at the legal clinic, another at the Forensic Medical Unit, and yet another meeting with a detective. The Family Justice Center has made a huge difference for our clients and their children.
>
> Jackie Dietz, Rady Children's Hospital

- Not all communities can do this

- Not all communities are ready

- Not all agencies want to play together

- A history of collaboration between diverse agencies is critical

- A history of interdisciplinary relationships is important

- Many communities may need to step back and work on the building blocks first

- Many need to dream big but start very small

Why will communities want to ignore these realities and move forward anyway? First, if money is available, every community will want to think they are ready. Second, it is hard to admit that your community is not doing good work with families in need. We want to be proud of our community. We want to celebrate all we do well and only want passing reference to our weaknesses as a city, a county, or a community. But we cannot talk about making Centers work until we step back a few steps and remember that no matter how exciting the concept, how powerful the potential result, and how positive the potential relationships between agencies, if our foundation is rotten, the house will not stand strong.

The experience in San Diego and elsewhere indicates that any

The proof that a Family Justice Center is successful is when cops and prosecutors can work together while still respecting their different roles. Success is when gay and lesbian-identified staff and pro-choice feminist advocates can work alongside pro-life, conservative evangelical chaplains and stay focused on the mission of helping those in need. The Family Justice Center concept will be successful if there is a shared value to let everybody be who they are while staying focused on the mission of providing the best possible services to victims in need.

William Lansdowne, Chief of Police
San Diego Police Department

community that cannot survive the assessment elements and the assessment questions should think long and hard before moving forward with plans for a Center. What can a community do to keep moving toward the vision even in incremental steps? Certain actions helped San Diego move forward toward the ultimate plan of co-located services with many diverse agencies. These actions can be considered and applied in other communities—whether rural, tribal, suburban, or urban—to lay the groundwork for a future Center.

ACTIONS TO PREPARE COMMUNITIES FOR CENTER VISION

Many of the actions listed below must be pursued in a community for years to prepare everyone. Others simply need to be instituted during the planning process, but they clearly support the process of developing consensus around the creation of a Center. If you conclude you are not ready to pursue immediate development, a slower, longer, evolutionary process will be the right course for your community. Consider these ideas for slowly moving your community closer to pursuing a Center:

• Get police and prosecutors talking to each other in weekly/ monthly roundtables about their handling of cases

• Get police and prosecutors in the same room with advocates to talk about the good and the bad of their work together on behalf of victims.

- Sit down and read some police reports together (with the names and addresses redacted) and discuss how cases are being handled and what should be happening in each set of facts

- Stop the finger pointing! Blaming each other for problems solves nothing!

- Create an open dialogue on each agency's views of system problems.

- Build one-on-one relationships and alliances, one friend at a time, with like-minded policy makers, elected officials, and community leaders.

- Look for opportunities for agencies to work together on individual cases.

- Ask victims and survivors what will serve them best—ask them what they need. Use focus groups. Use victim surveys— let them be anonymous! Ask victims that have experienced your system from different entry points—in shelters, in prosecutor's offices, in Family Court, in police departments, and in other community-based agencies.

- Identify how much money is being spent right now by all agencies and any other special domestic violence initiatives. Brainstorm how working together could make resources go further and save money on overhead or administrative expenses.

- Challenge everyone to think of the Center as a public safety initiative.

- Seek consensus on this principle: **We cannot protect children if we do not protect their mothers.**[9] If your child protection system will not agree with this principle, it should not be part of your Center. Alternatively, if a local child welfare system does accept this principle, they should be a critical component to a Family Justice Center.

- From the beginning, bring in those with a fresh perspective of concept evaluation—yes, the outside consultant who has experience with the Center model! The National Family Justice Center Alliance provides strategic planning assistance, consulting, and training to communities across the United States and around the world (www.familyjusticecenter.org)

- Consider using the services of a trained facilitator/strategic planner in evaluating your community's readiness.[10]

- Consider asking the Alliance to apply the FJC Snapshot Process Tool to your community—it is the most thorough assessment that can be done before opening an FJC. It costs some money and takes about three days but you end up with a report that can guide you toward opening or guide you toward the steps you need to take before you even begin planning a Center.

- Consider a pilot project involving co-located services if a small number of local agencies do have a strong history together and could form the nucleus for an initial experiment in living together (perhaps one day a week or one day a month). This model was successfully used in Salt Lake City, Utah by the YWCA when they first began their amazing Family Justice Center journey there.

- Consider building the Volkswagen before you try to build the Cadillac.

- Dream big, and start small if key partners are not willing to pursue the vision but other agencies are strongly supportive.

- Remember: Test all ideas and proposed pilot projects by asking victims and survivors to reflect with you on the viability and helpfulness of the proposed idea.

UNWILLING COMMUNITIES, AGENCIES, AND LEADERS

The last concept we must discuss as we acknowledge the difficulties in some communities in moving forward the idea of co-location is that some agencies and leaders just don't want to do it. They are un-

It makes perfect sense for the Child Advocacy Center to have staff at the Family Justice Center. The professionals from both the child abuse and domestic violence communities are seeing the same families. The lessons we've learned from working with children traumatized by abuse apply to children who witness domestic violence and vice versa. We learn from both systems and we apply them broadly. It's a win/win situation.

Charles Wilson, Director
Chadwick Center for Children and Families
Former Director, National Child Advocacy Center

willing to work through the issues, figure out the journey, and make co-location a reality for their hurting families. It comes in a few different forms.

I travel some places to speak or promote the vision for co-located services and someone comes up to me and says "I am opposed to family justice centers." They usually look pretty sour when they say it. I try to smile back and ask, "Are you opposed to asking victims how they would like to access services?" They always say they are not opposed to that. "Are you opposed to co-located services?" They always say they are not. "Are you opposed to the right of a victim to authorize the sharing of information with everyone that is trying to help her?" They always say they are not opposed if the victim authorizes it. "Are you supportive of providing multi-disciplinary services to victims?" They always say they support such an approach. So…I ask "What are you opposed to about family justice centers?" Some say they don't like the name, to which I respond use a different name…many communities have chosen something else. Some just keep dancing but others do get honest and articulate some issues worth briefly addressing.

THE HONEST ONES

I always appreciate the "opponents" of Family Justice Centers who are honest. There answers usually fall into about four categories: 1) Background checks; 2) Police departments or prosecutor's offices as the lead agency; 3) Potential competition for money; or 4) Difficulties communities have experienced trying to make Centers work well.

"Background Checks":

They say they are opposed to doing a background check on a victim before serving them. But when I say that Centers that serve men and women need to make sure they are not letting abusers in the door before they provide services, they agree that would be a really bad idea. When I note that some communities choose not to do background checks, that always surprises them. The point is: Each community must decide for themselves how this should work. Interestingly, they don't realize that victims at most Centers don't mind screening processes because they feel safer knowing that criminal defendants with active arrest warrants or pending cases of child abuse and domestic violence are not going to be in the kitchen or the playroom at their Center when they come forward for help.

Lead Agency Issues:

The second issue that often comes up from those that will honestly discuss their views of co-located services is that they don't want a certain agency or a certain individual to be in charge of their co-located model (if they are willing to pursue one). If I am talking to a shelter-based advocate, they will often say that cops and prosecutors are going to re-victimize victims and do bad things so they should not be part of a co-located model. But of course each community needs to decide for themselves whether public or private agencies are doing good work or not and whether they should be part of a co-located services model. In some cases, the local domestic violence shelter is not doing very good work and it will not be a good partner for other agencies. In other cases, a police department may be poorly investigating cases or arresting many victims and they should not be part of co-located services until those issues are addressed.

The decision about who the lead agency should be in any given community should always be decided by the community. Today, about half the Family Justice Centers or similar co-located service models that are affiliated with the National Family Justice Center Alliance are led by community-based domestic violence shelters or agencies. Many of them have been moving down the road of co-located services for years and the Family Justice Center concept has simply helped keep them moving forward, growing and evolving their model. About half the Centers are led by a public agency—a police department, a prosecutor's office, or a public health department. In those communities, it made the most sense given their funding streams, which agencies had the most respect from others, and which agencies were best able to bring others together.

Competition for Funds:

The third category of "opposition" to Family Justice Centers or other types of co-located service models is funding. Public safety initiatives tend to draw public support. Public safety is the highest priority of local government. If the cops and prosecutors get together with community partner agencies and push for a co-located services model, they have a great deal of clout. Public officials support them, businesses support them, and the community supports them. Existing agencies that often struggle for funding feel slighted, ignored, disrespected, or threatened. This is always an important topic in any community looking to create or expand a co-located services model. Will the effort take money away from existing programs? How can funding be pursued that does not damage an existing shelter or other critical, struggling local agencies?

We had this conversation at the national level when Family Justice Centers were added to the Violence Against Women Act by Congress in 2005. Advocates for shelters and sexual assault programs sought an agreement that co-located services would be added to Title I, historically referred to as the Grants to Encourage Arrest Program. All of us advocating for federal funding streams for local coordinated community response or co-located services model agreed. Any funding for co-located models should not come from other pots of money. It should come from the money currently accessed by police and prosecutors under Title I. This was a good example of the respect shown for shelter and community-based agencies even as the movement toward co-located services was gaining momentum.

Local communities should make every effort to work collaboratively when funding a co-location model. And if it is done right, it helps expand the pot of money either because local government is lobbied to increase spending on family violence or because partners find that it is easier to pursue funding together. Funders like collaborative approaches. They like efficiency. They like agencies that are willing share overhead expenses or prove they are committed to collaboration not isolated service delivery approaches.

Difficulties Of Others:

From time to time, I run into honest critics who say they don't believe in the co-located services model because they heard something about some Center or something went wrong in some community that pursued the concept. I try providing some perspective. We don't reject the idea of medical care because some hospital accidently cuts off the leg of the wrong patient. We don't reject the counseling profession because a therapist crosses a line and engages in an improper relationship with a client. We don't condemn all domestic violence shelters because some shelter suffers financial mismanagement or creates an oppressive environment for survivors. We sort out the good from the bad. We develop standards for best practices. We learn from the mistakes of others.

Co-located services are no different. There will be good and bad models. Some will thrive, others will struggle. Principles will emerge, leadership will matter, promising practices will be identified, and the journey will continue. We have had one Center close since the movement toward Family Justice Centers has emerged publicly. We have had over sixty open or expand from already existing co-location models. It is amazing more have not failed when most new start up non-profit entities do fail. There is little doubt that in the last seven years more small non-profit entities serving domestic violence victims have failed because of lack of financial support, poor management, or a failure to evolve and adapt to challenges than Family Justice Centers or other co-located service models.[11] But the challenges of some co-located services model should not lead the uninformed to say they "oppose" Family Justice Centers. How can anyone be against coordinated, effective, appropriate services for victims and their children if the victims want services in one location and a community is ready to do it?

CONCLUSION

The message to remember here is simple: Not all communities can or should pursue the Family Justice Center vision or any other co-located services vision unless they are ready and have key partners that are willing to figure out co-located services together. Communities with a history of mistrust, bad interagency relationships, or a lack of specialized intervention initiatives in domestic violence should not co-locate their existing services. Nothing could be worse for victims than incompetent, uninformed, and victim-endangering policies being enhanced by joining forces with other poorly trained and uninformed agencies. Local battered women's shelters and state domestic violence coalitions are often the best judges of the nature of interdisciplinary working relationships in a community. Such entities should play key roles in evaluating the appropriateness of the Family Justice Center model for a community.

If an assessment shows that the community is not ready, it can still take steps to move toward development of a Center in the future. Often, even if key partners are not ready to pursue the vision, other public and private agencies may pursue a pilot project or small co-located services initiative to advance the vision. The *dream big—start small* motto may be the best approach in communities where collaboration is an untested concept and potential unanticipated consequences have not been identified.

NOTES

1   See *The San Diego Story*, at: www.familyjusticecenter.org.

2   Ashley Walker, *Battered Women and the Law*, presentation for Cal Western School of Law course facilitated by Professor Gael Strack, January 2005.

3   The San Diego County Task Force on Domestic Violence Planning Committee played a powerful role in laying the groundwork for later collaboration. The 1988 members included: Murray Bloom, Director, San Diego Superior Court, Family Court Services; Lt. Commander Chuck Ertl, Ret., NAS Miramar; Joyce Faidley, Center for Women's Studies and Services (now known as Center for Community Solutions); Gene Fischer, Deputy Director, Family Service Center, MCRD; Dee Fuller, Director, District Attorney Victim Assistance Program; Betty White, Center for Community Solutions; Casey Gwinn, San Diego City Attorney's Office; Kate Yavenditti, San Diego Volunteer Lawyer's Program; Katy Lancaster, San Diego County Probation Department; Lee Lawless, family law attorney; Lt. Leslie Lord, San Diego Police Department; Elly Newman, Legal Advocate, YWCA Battered Women's Services; Ashley Walker, Director, YWCA Battered Women's Services; Ruth Hansen, San Diego County Probation Department; and Marilyn Cornell, San Diego County Probation Department.

4   See *supra*, *The San Diego Story*.

5   Casey G. Gwinn and Anne O'Dell, "Stopping the Violence: the Role of the Police Officer and the Prosecutor," *20 Western State University Law Review*, 1993, 298, 300-03.

6   Meredith Hofford and Adele V. Harrell, "Family Violence: Interventions for the Justice System," cited in *Battered Women and the Law*, Clare Dalton and Elizabeth M. Schneider, Foundation Press, New York, 2001, pp. 576-78.

7   Each of these questions can illuminate certain strengths and weaknesses in a community that will inform the discussion about a community's readiness to move forward with the Family Justice Center vision.

8   Interview with Sharon Denaro, December 8, 2005.

9   This principle will inform a community's ability to bring together child advocacy and domestic violence professionals. In the absence of this commitment, domestic violence advocates will find a child protective system far more likely to re-victimize battered women, prosecute victims of domestic violence for failure to protect, and fail to create a juvenile dependency system where batterers are held accountable for their violence against intimate partners in the context of identified child abuse allegations.

10 While many strategic planners will argue that subject matter knowledge is irrelevant to a planner or facilitator, I would argue that an experienced Family Justice Center planner from San Diego or from one of the other operating Centers around the country will be far more helpful than a facilitator with no knowledge of the vision you are considering. For more information on the role of a strategic planner, go to: www.startafamilyjusticecenter.org.

11 See Stephen R. Block, *Why Nonprofits Fail: Overcoming Founder's Syndrome,
    Fundphobia and Other Obstacles to Success*, Jossey-Bass (2008), for an excellent
    discussion on the stunning failure rate of non-profit organizations and the rea-
    sons for their failure to grow, evolve, and thrive.

CHAPTER FIVE

Build the Fence at the Top of the Cliff

Casey Gwinn and Gael Strack

Christina Jones was the mother of two beautiful children, Kayla, 4 months, and Kameron, 17 months. Christina loved to laugh and she loved to find humor in even tough situations. She also loved a man named Melvin Carter. Melvin Carter was violent and abusive and was convicted for assaulting her. The system in San Diego responded to him by prosecuting him in 2007 and placing him on probation. Later, he would be arrested again for assaulting Christina. But this time he was not prosecuted, the case was referred from the City Attorney's Office to the District Attorney's Office in order to save money. The District Attorney prepared paperwork for Melvin Carter to suffer a revocation of his probation for violating his terms by assaulting her again in 2009. Tragically, though, while the re-vocation proceedings were pending, Melvin Carter posted bail. The same day he got out of jail he came to Christina's house, held her hostage for hours, and then strangled her to death with her two young children pres-ent. He now faces life in prison for killing Christina. Their children will never see their mother again and their father will likely spend his life in prison, funded by the taxpayers of California. Sadly, Christina never got to the San Diego Family Justice Center. To date, there is no evidence that anyone referred her to the Center, attempted to transport her to the Center, or coordinated risk assessment, safety planning, and civil legal services at the Center.

As we held a vigil for Christina last December at the beach in Coronado, one of her favorite places, I told her parents that we would never forget Christina. Her death was such a tragedy and the San Diego intervention system did not work as well as it should have. Melvin Carter should never have gotten out of jail. Christina should have had a whole busload of people working to get her services at the San Diego Family Justice Center. All the agencies at the Center should have been working together to ensure her safety and his accountability. But we failed. So, the money is being spent at the bottom of the cliff and Christina is not playing in a park somewhere with her children far from the edge of that cliff. She is dead.

WHY NOT BUILD FENCES AT THE TOP OF THE CLIFF?

As we have done this work across America and around the world, we often make the point that it is cheaper to build a fence at the top of a cliff than it is to send ambulances to the bottom of the cliff. It is a simple word picture that encapsulates years of research on the importance of prevention and the high cost of intervention. But it is still hard to get through to many elected officials. Most of the time public officials don't understand the true cost of domestic violence. This chapter is devoted to providing the data for communities to educate their elected officials on the cost effectiveness of building the fence at the top of the cliff instead of sending ambulances to the bottom of the cliff.

THE CENTER IS WORTH THE MONEY

Any community considering development of a Family Justice Center must invariably address the financial issues that come with pursuing such a vision. Is the cost of a Center worth it? Will it save money in the long run? In a world of scarce resources, is a Center a wise investment of money? Sadly, most communities have never done the evaluation necessary to determine if co-located services are cost-effective and therefore financially viable. But in San Diego, Alameda County, New York City, and many other Family Justice Center communities, we have done the analysis and the news is good. The Center is worth the money. If it saved one life, it would be worth it morally and financially. But it can save far more than one life.

In New York, Mayor Michael Bloomberg took the lead in launching three regional Family Justice Centers. Since January 2002, Commissioner Yolanda B. Jimenez, in the Mayor's Office to Combat Domestic Violence, has led the way. Mayor Bloomberg also created the New York City Family Justice Center Initiative which is a private/public partnership of the Mayor's Fund to Advance New York City, a 501(c)(3) not-for-profit organization established to promote partnerships between the City and the private sector.

The Family Justice Center Initiative is part of the Bloomberg Administration's overall effort to reduce domestic violence and provide comprehensive services to victims. As a result of the City's focus on this issue, family related crimes have declined by 21% and intimate partner homicides have declined by 51% citywide over the last six years.[1] In Alameda County, District Attorney Nancy O'Malley and other officials have credited the Family Justice Center and its related collaborations and initiatives with reducing domestic violence homicides by 75%.[2]

> The Family Justice Center model is, at its core, a concept that increases community capacity while also providing diverse, culturally competent services to victims and their children from a single location. It is common sense that such an approach, if executed properly, will provide greater assistance to those in need.
>
> Mary Beth Buchanan, Former Director
> Office on Violence Against Women
> U.S. Department of Justice

San Diego has reported similar declines since pursuing co-located services in the early 1990's.[3] After the official opening of the Family

Justice Center, the decline continued. Since the opening of the Center, domestic violence homicides have been reduced by approximately 50%.[4] While homicide rates are difficult to measure or compare from year to year in smaller communities, there is clear evidence that wrapping victims in support and services reduces lethality, reduces risk of re-offense, and increases offender accountability.[5]

We will spend some time in this chapter on the general cost estimates of domestic violence for society and for the criminal justice system. Then we will look at the minimal costs of running a Center. But before we do that, let's be frank. As soon as supporters start talking about a Center, they are going to hear it all:

- We need a federal grant.

- We don't have enough money in our community to support even our existing programs.

- We cannot do this without more financial support from the state.

- We are cutting programs right now—we cannot add another one.

- If we had strong leaders in this community, we could do it, but our Police Chief does not support our work to stop domestic violence.

- I am just a PTA President; I have no power to make something like this happen here.

- I'm a pastor, not a politician.

- No one will listen to me if I start pushing for this in our town because I am a homemaker.

- I'm a judge—this is not my job.

- Our District Attorney isn't even prosecuting these cases; everything gets plea bargained or dismissed.

- Maybe we will have our act together some day and can do this kind of Center, but we just are not ready right now.

We will touch on some of these lies, excuses, and half-truths in the pages that follow. But what is the number one answer to why leaders will say there cannot be a Center? *We cannot afford it.*

And the main message of this chapter? *Building the fence at the top of the cliff is always cheaper than sending really fast ambulances to the bottom of the cliff.*

THE TRUTH ABOUT PRIORITIES, VALUES, AND RESOURCES

If you have stayed with the book this long, it is probably time to speak the cold hard truth about priorities, values, and resources in our communities, our country, and our world. We are all responsible for family violence. Batterers get away with their violence because our communities let them. Battered women don't get the help they need because we don't provide it. We clamor for better schools, newer roads, nicer parks, and lower taxes. We clamor for an end to hostilities in the Middle East when a soldier loses his life. But we don't clamor for Family Justice Centers or co-located service models for victims of abuse.

> The FJC is a wonderful place for victims. Whoever thought of this is a wonderful person! The staff were an awesome help to my family and saved me a lot of time. When I walked in I felt a burden being released from my shoulders. Now I can have peace of mind.
>
> Sandra, Ouachita Parish Family Justice Center Client (Monroe, LA), 2009

We don't picket politicians who fail to make family violence a priority. We settle for a few dollars here and there in our community-based social service organizations from local government. We watch our local, state, and federal government spend millions and even billions on water and sewer systems, airports, mass transit systems, public employee pensions, public safety services, redevelopment projects, the military, subsidized airline travel, financial aid to other countries, and a host of other priorities. We call for more resources to build prisons and put more police officers on the street to protect us from gangs, street violence, and even consumer fraud. But we don't demand the same level of support from our governments and social institutions to stop family violence. We tolerate it. We become silent co-conspirators with those who continue to visit violence on their families.

Martin Luther King, Jr. said it many years ago. His context and topic were different, but his point was well-taken: "We in this generation must repent, not only for the words and deeds of the bad people but for the appalling silence of the good people." His indictment still rings true today in a country saturated with family violence. When was the last time you engaged in civil disobedience to protest a judge's mistreatment of domestic violence victims in court? When was the last time you wrote a letter to the editor demanding the elected officials step up and do something to stop family violence? When was the last time you called a local elected official to urge proactive effort to reduce violence in the home? When was the last time you heard a politician say, "We cannot afford these new programs for domestic violence victims and their children," and you stood up and replied, "Liar, liar, pants on fire!"

Most of the money we spend on the criminal justice system in this country is spent too late. We often say it: "In America, we raise our criminals at home." The vast majority of men and women that we lock up in this country for all crimes came from homes with domestic violence, child abuse, drug abuse, or alcohol abuse. The vast majority of criminals in this country grew up in violent and abusive homes. Dr. Mark Cunningham and Dr. Mark Vigen have documented the family of origin issues with virtually all death row inmates.[6] They write: "Many if not most death row inmates have histories of paternal abandonment, foster care and institutionalization, abuse and neglect, and/or parental substance abuse... The presence of pathological family interactions in the histories of capital murderers is consistent with an extensive body of research demonstrating the role of disrupted attachment and disturbed family relationships in the etiology of violence."[7] But instead of dealing with it and preventing the criminal conduct to begin with, we wait and spend our money later. The National Institute of Justice has estimated the total cost of personal crime in the United States to be $105 billion per year.[8] And they acknowledge that this likely undercounts crimes of domestic violence and rape because of low reporting rates! The most comprehensive study of its kind, released in 2007, found that violence costs the United States $70 billion annually[9].

So, whatever study you rely on, we are spending the money. We just spend it way too late. We have learned to send ambulances to the bottom of the cliff instead of building fences at the top of the cliff. We wait until the children of domestic violence grow up and move on to populate our juvenile halls and adult prisons. We spend the money then! We don't spend it stopping the violence before lives are deeply scarred.

THE TRUTH ABOUT RESOURCES

Not only do the resources exist in our culture to help victims and proactively implement programs to stop family violence, but we are presently paying millions to deal with what we are not stopping. Consider this: In 2004, the San Diego County Health and Human Services Department engaged in an evaluation to determine how much money the criminal justice system spent on each domestic violence homicide in our county. The result: Each one costs the system approximately $2.5 million, including the cost of lifetime incarceration for the killer.[10] The table below shows the exact breakdown of those numbers from the Health Department.

COST PER DOMESTIC VIOLENCE HOMICIDE IN SAN DIEGO COUNTY

	Cost
Four police responses	$1,582
Two temporary restraining orders	1,400

	Cost
180-day jail term	19,292
Two years' probation	4,104
One emergency room visit	855
Two weeks in a domestic violence shelter	2,094
One week at Polinsky Center for three children	4,200
One year of foster care for three children	18,756
Two coroner's autopsies	5,510
Homicide investigation/court system prosecution	1,500,000
State prison sentence	1,000,000
TOTAL	**$2,557,793**

Intra-familial homicide was estimated to cost this country $1.7 billion annually, according to research by Murray Straus in 1986.[11] The National Institute of Justice estimates the average cost at $2.4 million per domestic violence homicide. An analysis conducted by Miami-Dade County[12] determined the cost of 62 local domestic violence homicides per year averaged $500,000 per homicide. That estimate, however, did not include services to survivors and families, dependency proceedings regarding termination of parental rights, and long-term costs of incarceration.

Clearly, these numbers do not take into account the human costs of pain and suffering. When you think of the brutal (and preventable) murder of so many victims across the country and around the globe, the hard costs described above barely register. We can't help but think about the pain and suffering of a victim's family and friends. In one study conducted in England by Professor Sylvia Walby, the costs of pain and human suffering were estimated at 17 billion pounds (approximately $30 billion U.S. dollars).[13]

So we are spending the money. We are spending it on other things, and we are spending it at the wrong time. We wait until the victim is dead, the family is destroyed, and the children are scarred for life before we spend the largest amounts of money to address the issue.

But think about the money that local communities expend in the criminal justice system now on domestic violence cases even if the victim does not die. We spend millions in this country providing temporary restraining orders, enforcing those orders, processing misdemeanor and felony cases, issuing warrants of arrest, incarcerating abusers, managing public work service for offenders, funding halfway houses, bringing repeat offenders back to court over and over again. Filing cases and then dismissing them because we don't have the evidence or we don't share information among all the agencies that do have the evidence.

Just the costs of investigation, prosecution and incarceration for arrests and prosecutions of non-homicide domestic violence cases are staggering. Joan Zorza identified the issue in her article, "Women Battering: High Costs and the State of the Law,"[14] when she pointed out that domestic violence incidents are the largest category of calls to police each year. One-third of all police time is spent responding to domestic violence calls.[15]

The New York City Police Department made 12,724 domestic violence arrests in 1989 at an average cost of $3,241 per arrest. Although the cost of indigent defense attorneys was not included, the city paid at least $41 million in police services, court costs, and detention time arising from domestic violence arrests. The National Institute of Justice estimates that 15% of all law enforcement costs are due to domestic violence, totaling $67 billion per year.[16] Of course, not all reported intimate partner incidents result in arrest. In San Diego, only 33% of such cases result in an arrest.[17]

It is no wonder the estimates are in the millions and even billions when you multiply these numbers times every crime and every criminal—most of whom, as noted earlier, have come from homes with drugs, alcohol, domestic violence, and child abuse!

BUSINESS COMMUNITY AND TAXPAYERS FOOT THE BILL

The business community often thinks domestic violence has nothing to do with them. But in 2007, CAEPV, Liz Claiborne and Safe Horizon released a groundbreaking survey on corporate executives and employee awareness of the impact of domestic violence in the workplace. The survey shows that… only 13% of corporate executives think their companies should address the problem.[18]But the research is compelling. Let's look at what we know about the cost of family violence to the business community and the tax paying public. Research has confirmed over and over the impact on employees experiencing family violence, including:

• Loss of productivity

• Higher stress

• Increased absenteeism

• Increased employee turnover

• Higher health care costs

• Reduced staff morale

The cost of a violence epidemic that most CEOs and corporate executives don't think really impacts them is enormous to American businesses. The Bureau of National Affairs has estimated the cost at $3 to 6 billion. These costs are not simply due to lost productivity or increased medical costs. The violence does come to work. In one study, while five percent of all places of work, including state and local governments, had a violent incident, half of the largest businesses (employing 1,000 or more workers) reported an incident. In these largest companies, domestic violence made up 24.1 percent of all violent incidents. Of all businesses reporting an incident of workplace violence in the previous 12 months, 21 percent reported that the incident affected the fear level of their employees and 21 percent indicated that the incident affected their employees' morale.[19]

In surveys conducted by Kim Wells and the Corporate Alliance

"Thank you for giving so much of yourselves to this work. For myself, many past wounds were brought to the light, some for the first time. And though this has been quite painful, the process is bringing life back into the deadest places. Thank God. I pray that your ability to shed light and truth onto hurting women will grow even more. Your work is not wasted!"

"Although there are many individual in the community who have made this ordeal tolerable, those I have mentioned in this letter have left a positive memory, touched our lives, and continue to be instrumental in our healing. Each of them linked and connected to us by each other—a true reflection of the effect of the Family Violence Project and your commitment to bring agencies together under one roof and provide timely and continuous support to victims of violence."

"Our society is truly greater with these community leaders going the extra mile to provide safety and support to victims like my family. I have felt truly comforted by their ongoing compassion and concern."

Exit Interview Quotes from Anonymous Clients 2009
Family Violence Project—Mosaic Counselling and Family Services Center
Waterloo Region—Ontario, Canada

to End Partner Violence, sixty-four percent (64%) of victims of domestic violence indicated that their ability to work was affected by the violence. Among key causes for their decline in productivity, victims noted "distraction" (57%); "fear of discovery" (45%); "harassment by intimate partner at work (either by phone or in person)" (40%); fear of intimate partner's unexpected visits" (34%); "inability to complete assignments on time" (24%); and "job loss" (21%).

According to the CDC, intimate partner violence victims lose a total of nearly 8.0 million days of paid work—the equivalent of more than 32,000 full-time jobs.[20]Battered women incur an estimated $24 million a year in medical expenses, much of which is paid by employer-sponsored health care plans.[21]

Homicide was the second leading cause of death on the job for women in 2003, according to the Bureau of Labor Statistics' (BLS) Census of Fatal Occupational Injuries (CFOI) system data. Fifteen percent (15%) of the 119 workplace homicides of women in that year were attributed to a current or former husband or boyfriend. Seventy-four percent of employed battered women are harassed by abusive husbands and partners at work.[22]

Unaddressed domestic violence in the workplace poses a safety risk to other employees as well. It is not always the victim who is shot or killed. We even have a phrase for it based on the number of postal workers with domestic violence histories who have killed a mate or coworker. We call it "going postal." We should not pick on the U.S. Postal Service, though. It is everywhere. According to the National Safe Working Place Institute, in 1994 over 40% of workplace homicides were perpetrated by men with a history of violence against women. In another study, one-third of workplace homicides were family violence-related.[23]

DIVING DEEPER INTO THE COSTS

The first step to measuring cost is to determine the true prevalence of domestic violence in society. The 2003 report published by the Centers for Disease Control and Prevention, *Costs of Intimate Partner Violence Against Women in the United States*, pointed out the struggles with gathering the statistics and determining the prevalence of domestic violence.[24] It cited lack of consensus about terminology, variations in survey methodology, gaps in data collection, different time frames, the reluctance to report victimization, the repetitive nature of domestic violence, limited populations, and survey limitations. According to the 2008 NCVS [National Crime Victimization Survey], victims reported 47% of violent crimes… to the police.[25] Other studies suggest the number of unreported cases could be as high as 98%.[26]

WHAT IS THE PREVALENCE?

Recognizing these challenges, we must start somewhere and accept that, by any measure, estimated costs are conservative. A minimum of 1.3 million women are victims of physical assault by an intimate partner each year.[27] In many studies, as noted, the numbers are much higher. Around the world, the numbers could be enormous depending on the studies you look at. In one recent study, up to 71% of women had been beaten, sexually abused, or otherwise abused at some time during their lifetime![28] A California study estimated that approximately 700,000 women in California are victims of domestic violence over a 12-month period, which represents only one-third of the criminal cases reported to the California Department of Justice by law enforcement agencies in a year.[29]

When it comes to homicides, an average of more than three women and one man are murdered every day as a result of domestic violence in this country. In 1999, 1,642 murders were attributed to domestic violence, and 1,218 of the victims were women.[30] As we write, there is strong evidence to believe that in 2009 domestic violence murders rose across the United States. Utah, the first state to report domestic violence homicides has reported a 30% increase in homicides from 2008.[31]

> The FJC is a wonderful place for victims. Whoever thought of this is a wonderful person! The staff members were an awesome help to my family and saved me a lot of time. When I walked in I felt a burden being released from my shoulders. Now I can have peace of mind.
>
> Sandra, Ouachita Parish Family Justice Center Client (Monroe, LA), 2009

WHAT ABOUT HEALTH CARE COSTS?

Domestic violence also inflicts major costs on the health care system. About half of all female victims report an injury of some kind, and about 20% of them seek medical assistance.[32] It is estimated that one million women seek medical care for abuse-related injuries in the United States each year.[33] The American Medical Association estimates that 28% of women seen in ambulatory clinics have been battered at some time during their lives.[34] Approximately 20 to 25% of pregnant women seeking prenatal care are experiencing intimate partner violence.[35] It has been reported that as high as 37.6% of the women in a sample of pregnant adolescents were experiencing domestic violence.[36] Battered women account for 25% of women who attempt suicide and 25% of women using a psychiatric emergency service.[37] One study determined that approximately 63% of female psychiatric inpatients had a history of physical abuse, the majority of which was inflicted by adults sharing their home.[38]

> There was a lot of emotional and physical abuse. A lot of fighting that would progress into a kind of physical fighting. I don't know what I would have done if the family justice center wouldn't have been here. To look at where my life was two years ago versus now, it's really amazing and I would say thank you so much.
>
> Jana, Nampa Family Justice Center Client (Nampa, ID), 2008

In *Guidelines for the Health Care of Intimate Partner Violence for California Health Care Professionals*, Dr. Connie Mitchell looked at the health care financial impact of this large amount of domestic violence. She cited the costs of both medical care and lost days of productivity related to domestic violence between *$3 and $10 billion annually.*[39] She reported on a study that compared health care costs for victims of partner violence with non-victims in a large Midwest health plan and found victims incurred $1,775 more in health care costs in a single year of study than non-victims did.

The Pennsylvania Blue Shield Initiative estimated that domestic violence health care costs to the state are $326.6 million per year, which, if extrapolated nationwide, would amount to over $6.5 billion annually.[40] This figure does not include mental health costs related to the abuse of women nor the fact that many women's injuries are never connected to prior abuse. Nor does it take into account that battered women are 15.3 times more likely than non-battered women to seriously consider suicide and battering is the single greatest context identified for—and possibly associated with—half of female alcoholism.[41]

Are you getting tired yet? We are not done. There are more costs being passed on by businesses to consumers and passed on by government to the taxpayers.

WHAT ABOUT SHELTER COSTS?

California alone has approximately 112 shelters, 94 of which have received state and federal funding through the state Office of Criminal Justice Planning and the federal Department of Health Services (DHS).[42] Emergency domestic violence shelters in California work within tight funding restrictions, which limit the length of stay to 30 to 45 days. According to data gathered by DHS, in the year 2000, 80,000 women received services at shelters while 23,388 individuals were turned away because the shelter was full. [43] Between 2000 and 2003, DHS funded 91 shelters, awarding each of them between $150,000 and $190,000 annually. The average total annual shelter budget was determined to be $1,231,910. These shelters received a total of approximately 266,000 calls to their hotlines in a one-year period. The annual budget for one California shelter completely supported by private funds was $2,686,65.[44]

In addition to emergency shelters, many communities may have

At one time I believed the person I was sharing a life with was my spiritual leader and soul mate. After 10 years of brainwashing in a secluded and controlled environment, I no longer was thriving but slowly being tortured in such a subtle way that I thought there was something wrong with me. Even after my family and friends were no longer allowed, after being pushed around so much that I hurt all over, after hiding weapons for self-defense around the house, I continued to believe the lie that I might be crazy.

One morning I heard an ad on the radio that asked a series of questions, to which I answered yes to all. At the end of the commercial the prompter said if the answer is yes to even just one of those questions, you might be a victim of domestic violence. I memorized the safe number to call and the safe voice on the other end told me about the Family Justice Center and how to safely get help. They have taught me and my children how to be safe, connect to legal services, and find a support group with others who understand. The agencies at the Center help me realize more and more every day that it is not our fault. They have helped me break free from the cycle of violence and enter the circle of hope and healing.

Lydia, Knoxville Family Justice Center Client
(Knoxville, TN), 2010

their own facility for transitional housing for domestic violence victims and their children. In San Diego alone, there are 12 such facilities.[45] Many receive public funding, a cost borne by the taxpayers. If
there was truly a way to stop the violence and stop the next generation
of victims, it would indeed change the world!

WHAT ABOUT ANIMAL ABUSE?

There is a growing recognition that domestic violence, child
abuse, and animal abuse often occur in the same households.[46] Frank
Ascione found that nearly two-thirds of battered women seeking shelter in safe houses report that their abuser threatened to harm or actually harmed or killed their pet[47]. Witnessing this type of abuse can
be devastating to anyone, especially children. Battered women and
their children have a tendency to worry about the safety of their pets
and sometimes are reluctant to leave an abusive situation because of
them.[48] Needless to say, there are significant costs associated with the
investigation and prosecution of animal abuse cases, the sheltering
of pets, animal shelters, and vet bills. Though no studies have been
conducted on these costs, we should at least note them.

WHAT ABOUT LITIGATING DIVORCES AND CHILD CUSTODY PROCEEDINGS?

According to the 2009 National Vital Statistics Report, the nation's divorce rate was 3.5 divorces per 1,000.[49]Many involved children; millions of children across America have experienced the pain,
confusion, and grief that result from divorce,[50] in addition to an ugly,
costly custody battle. The consequences for children depend on the
degree of parental conflict prior to divorce.[51] In domestic violence
cases, the conflict may likely continue after separation, causing even
more pain to children. Fatality reviews and inquests around the world
point dramatically to the increased risk when abused women and
children attempt to leave their batterer. In 1996, the rate of spousal
homicide for separated women was 79 per one million, compared
with 3 per one million for married women. This statistic clearly sug-

gests that separation can be a particularly dangerous time for women, which is consistent with the definition of domestic violence as abuse of power and control.[52]

> Todo estubo exelente. Me sentoi protegida, bespetada y pode enterarme de mis derechos como madre que ignoraba la Senoirita Angela fue muy amabil y me hablo con Onestidad y respecto Gracias Angela. Everything was excellent. I felt protected and respected. I learned about my rights as a mother. Miss Angela was very kind. She spoke to me with honesty and respect. Thank you, Angela."
>
> Guadalupe, San Diego Family Justice Center Client, 2005

Batterers are also twice as likely as non-batterers to apply for custody of children.[53] Their fight for custody and visitation rights, as a way to further control victims, increases the costs of litigation and drains the financial resources of abused victims. Often the family courts rely on custody evaluators and mediators to help them make these determinations, and access to children after separation may require specialized supervision facilities to protect both the children and victimized parents from ongoing abuse. Court costs and the costs for supervised visitation centers must be added to the overall cost of domestic violence, along with the costs of child abduction and child homicides. Again, the costs of the family court system in processing the enormous number of family violence cases has not been calculated, but the numbers are clearly substantial.

So how do these costs compare with running a Center that reduces homicides and reduces repeat offenses against women and children? Simply, the cost of one homicide is more than $1 million in any community in America. In many communities, the cost is much higher when you factor in long-term incarceration for the killer. So what is the cost of running a Center?

THE COST OF RUNNING A FAMILY JUSTICE CENTER

In contrast to the already existing costs of domestic violence described above, Center costs are minimal. When compared to the financial impacts of domestic violence on the business community and the health care system, a Center, with all costs included, becomes an overwhelmingly cost-efficient service delivery model.

For purposes of making a financial case for a Center, let's use the National Institute of Justice estimate of $2.4 million per domestic violence homicide as we frame the costs of operating a Center. The operating cost of the San Diego Family Justice Center is $1,000,000 a year for two floors of office space, approximately 22,000 square feet, parking, utilities and a staff of six. In the first eight years of operation, the City of San Diego saw a nearly 50% drop in domestic violence homicides (from nine in 2002 to three in 2008). While we readily acknowledge the complexity of shifting costs in the criminal justice system from the back end to the front end, there can be little argument that preventing homicides is right morally and financially.

In later chapters, we will talk about outcomes in Centers but New York City Mayor Michael Bloomberg has tied the Brooklyn Family Justice Center with a nearly 50% drop in domestic violence homicides since the Center has opened.[54] Even the most conservative cost estimates for the cost of handling and prosecuting a murder in New York City would far exceed the costs involved in organizing, funding, and managing the Brooklyn, Queens, and Bronx Family Justice Centers.[55]

The partner agencies are, of course, major beneficiaries of the

For decades, police officers have responded to calls, sent the case to a detective for follow up, and shipped the case off to the prosecutor's office. It is an arduous process and very costly for a partial solution. It is clear now that it is not enough. The full picture of domestic violence in a family cannot be addressed without advocates, civil attorneys, social service providers, doctors, nurses, counselors, chaplains, community volunteers, and many others. The victim needs all of us to work together to ensure the arrest and the prosecution is going to help stop the violence, giving the victim and her children safety, hope, and healing long after the criminal case is over. If we all work together, arrests and the prosecutions will go down and in the long run we will save a great deal of money while saving lives.

Lt. Lori Luhnow, Director, San Diego Family Justice Center

I really felt comfortable with everyone around here, because they under-stood me and didn't judge me. The FJC is the best! Such positive energy! What a very welcoming center.

Patricia, Hillsborough County Family Justice Center Client, 2009

funding for the building or buildings for Centers in a community. Partner agencies save rent money and overhead expenses by coming to a Center where those costs will be paid by the lead agency. As an example, San Diego's Chadwick Center estimated that hosted office space at the San Diego Family Justice Center saved them approximately 15% of the total budget for operating their Family Violence Program, which included eleven full-time staff members.[56]

Sample Operating Costs for Other Centers

The Nampa (ID) Family Justice Center has an operating budget of $587,000. Nampa has a mix of funding sources including public funds, grants, reimbursable funds from services provided, and private funds.

Operating costs in a smaller Center or in a Center operating out of an existing domestic violence shelter are much lower. The Ouachita Parish Family Justice Center in Monroe (LA) costs approximately $196,000 to operate as a "program" of the Wellspring, the shelter-based organization that leads it. Local elected officials regularly hail the investment of public dollars in the operation of their Family Justice Center as extremely cost-effective compared to the cost of dealing with higher death rates and higher recidivism rates.[57]

The Bexar County Family Justice Center reports annual rent of $132,000 to cover almost 11,000 square feet ($1.04 a square foot). The landlord is University Health System, a local public hospital owned by the County. The administrative arm (including a client service coordinator, office manager, program manager, IT manager, administrative assistant, two intake workers, and an executive director) is approximately $500,000 and is paid by out of the District Attorney's budget. The partner agencies absorb their own staffing costs and incidental expenses.

The measurable financial benefit of the co-located services model for community-based non-profit agencies is the money saved in leasing, overhead, or rent costs that end up being absorbed by the lead agency for the co-location model. We will talk later about a "pay to play" approach where partner agencies are required to pay rent to the lead agency. We strongly oppose such a model and it negatively impacts the direct financial incentive to partner agencies to co-locate.

Other Key Factors in the Costs of Operation

Operating costs in a Center vary greatly depending on whether they must purchase a facility, rent space, or obtain rent-free office space from city or county government. Most Centers dream too small at the beginning and often have to add space for more partner agencies in a second or third phase of their project—this too adds cost. Centers that have to rent indefinitely spend more than those that can buy a building or have the government provide a building. But costs of operation still pale in comparison to the financial savings from reductions in homicides, recidivism, court costs, medical expenses, shelter costs, workplace-related violence, and other expenses. Operating a rural, suburban, or urban Center is not creating a bureaucracy. It is efficiently bringing together those who already work in the field and magnifying their effectiveness for the benefit of hurting families and the community.

CONCLUSION

The money is there to develop Centers across America. Local, state, and federal governments spend it now—but they spend it too late. Businesses spend billions now to deal with family violence—but they spend it too late. So many not only spend it, but they spend it over and over as the cycle of violence repeats itself from generation to generation.

To begin to change the spending priorities of government and the private sector, we must reject the lie that there are not enough resources to create Family Justice Centers. Once we refuse to buy the lie, we can start talking about the reallocation of scarce resources. We can start talking about promoting peace at home in order to have peace abroad. We can start talking about ways to export our Center vision for healing families in the United States and around the world by stopping violence in the home.

Even in San Diego, our system has a long ways to go. Christina needed our help long before her murderer was prosecuted. We failed her. Perhaps, in her memory, the next time you hear someone say we cannot afford to develop Centers, you can say "Liar, liar, pants on fire!" We believe it would make Christina smile.

NOTES

1   See http://www.webhse.com/pdfs/2008.07.18-01_nyc_queens.pdf.

2   See http://www.acfjc.org/files/acfjcinfosheet.pdf.

3   The City of San Diego reported 30 domestic violence homicides in 1985. Seventeen years later, after a host of initiatives including co-located services initiatives, the City of San Diego had 9 domestic violence homicides the year before the San Diego Family Justice Center opened.

4   In 2002, the City of San Diego had 9 domestic violence homicides using the definition of domestic violence contained in California Penal Code section 13700. By 2008, the City of San Diego reported 3 domestic violence homicides.

5   Critics of any arguments about effectiveness always point out that there is no way to control for all the variables in a community when analyzing homicide rates or causative reasons for increases or decreases. Rural and suburban communities may have a spike or large variations in domestic violence homicides from year to year. Larger population bases make tracking trends easier but it is still difficult to point to direct causative links to increases or decreases.

6   Cunningham, Vigen, "Death Row Inmate Characteristics, Adjustment, and Confinement: A Critical Review of the Literature," Behav. Sci. Law 20: 191–210 (2002)

7   Id.

8   See 1996 NIJ Research Report, "Victim Costs and Consequences: A New Look", at http://www.ncjrs.gov/pdffiles/victc ost.pdf

9   Corso PS, Mercy JA, Simon TR, Finkelstein EA, & Miller TR. *"Medical Costs and Productivity Losses Due to Interpersonal Violence and Self- Directed Violence"*, *American Journal of Preventive Medicine, 2007: 32(6): 474-482.*

10 To view a power point presentation of the San Diego HHS Study, go to www.familyjusticecenter.org and log-in to the Resource Library to view the slides. The report is entitled: *San Diego County Fatality Review Committee Report*, Department of Human Health & Human Services.

11 Dr. Connie Mitchell, *Guidelines for the Health Care of Intimate Partner Violence for California Health Professionals*, California Medical Training Center, 2004, p. 17.

12 Jennifer Glazer Moon, research memo prepared in 2005 for Miami, Dade County, FL, conducting a feasibility study for the creation of a Family Justice Center.

13 See   www.equalities.gov.uk/pdf/Summ%20cost%20of%20domestic%20violence%20Sep%2004.pdf

14 Joan Zorza, "Women Battering: High Costs and the State of the Law," *Clearinghouse Review,* 1994 Special Issue, pp. 383-88.

15 Ibid.

16 Supra, Bugarin, *Prevalence.*

17 Kate Sproul, *California's Response to Domestic Violence: A History of Policy Issues*

and Legislative Actions to Combat Domestic Violence in California, California
Senate Office of Research, June 2003.

18 See http://www.caepv.org/getinfo/facts_stats.php?factsec=3)

19 See *The Survey of Workplace Violence Prevention, Bureau of Labor Statistics, October 2006.*

20 See *Costs of Intimate Partner Violence Against Women in the United States, U.S.
Centers for Disease Control. Report released April 28, 2003.*

21 L. Greenfeld et al., *Violence by Intimates: Analysis of Data on Crimes by Current or Former Spouses, Boyfriends and Girlfriends,* U. S. Department of Justice,
1998.

22 U.S. Dept. of Justice, 1999.

23 *Workplace Violence: A Report to the Nation.* University of Iowa Injury Prevention Research Center, Iowa City, IA, 2001.

24 *Costs of Intimate Partner Violence Against Women in the United States,* report by
Department of Health and Human Services, Centers for Disease Control and
Prevention, Atlanta, GA, 2003.

25 See http://bjs.ojp.usdoj.gov/content/pub/pdf/cv08.pdf

26 R. Emerson Dobash and Russell Dobash, *Violence Against Wives,* The Free
Press, 1979.

27 See http://www.ncadv.org/files/DomesticViolenceFactSheet(National).pdf)

28 See http://www.who.int/gender/violence/who_multicountry_study/Chapter3-
Chapter4.pdf)

29 Alicia Bugarin, *The Prevalence of Domestic Violence in California,* California
Research Bureau, November 2002.

30 *Intimate Partner Violence and Age of Victim,* Bureau of Justice Statistics Special
Report, October 2001.

31 See http://www.fox13now.com/news/kstu-domestic-violence-homicides,0,39
57835.story. These statistics are compiled annually by the Utah Domestic Violence Council. The report shows 27 homicides in 2009, 22 homicides in 2008,
and 18 homicides in 2007.

32 *National Crime Victimization Survey, 1992-96,* study of injured victims of violence, 1994.

33 Commonwealth Fund, *1998 Survey of Women's Health.*

34 P. Salber and E. Taliaferro, *The Physician's Guide to Domestic Violence: How to
Ask the Right Questions and Recognize Abuse,* Volcano Press, Volcano, CA, 1995,
p. 9.

35 Ibid., p. 10.

36 M. Curry et al., "Effects of Abuse on Maternal Complications and Birth
Weight in Adult and Adolescent Women," *Obstetrics & Gynecology,* 1998, 92,4,
pp. 530-34.

37 Salber and Taliaferro, p. 9.

38 Ibid.

39 P. Tjaden et al., *Comparing Violence Over the Life Span in Samples of Same-Sex
and Opposite Sex Cohabitants.*

40   Zorza, *Clearing House Review.*
41   Ibid.
42   Bugarin., *Prevalence.*
43   Ibid.
44   Ibid.
45   Presentation by the Shelter Committee of the San Diego Domestic Violence Council, November 2005.
46   B. Boat, "The Relationship Between Violence to Children and Violence to Animals," *Journal of Interpersonal Violence,* 1995, Vol. 10, p. 229-35.
47   Frank Ascione, "Battered Women's Report of Their Partners' and Their Children's Cruelty to Animals," *Journal of Emotional Abuse,* 1998, Vol. 1, pp. 119-33.
48   L. Kogan et al., "Crosstrails: a Unique Foster Program to Provide Safety for Pets of Women in Safe Houses," *Violence Against Women,* April 2004, Vol. 10, No. 4, p. 418.
49   See http://www.cdc.gov/nchs/fastats/divorce.htm.
50   P. Jaffe et al., *Child Custody & Domestic Violence—A Call for Safety and Accountability.* Sage Publications, Thousand Oaks, CA, 2003.
51   Ibid.
52   Ibid.
53   Janet Bowermaster, "Relocation Custody Disputes Involving Domestic Violence," *University of Kansas Law Review,* 1998, 46 (3), p. 433-63.
54   See http://www.webhse.com/pdfs/2008.07.18-01_nyc_queens.pdf for more information about Mayor Bloomberg's amazing vision and leadership in creating Centers in boroughs across New York City.
55   Mayor Michael Bloomberg has demonstrated clearly how much leadership matters in the Family Justice Center movement. He regularly speaks about the Centers, meets regularly with Commissioner Yolanda Jimenez, the Coordinator of the Mayor's Office to Combat Domestic Violence, and continues to dedicate the resources necessary to make each of the Centers a success.
56   Interview with Charles Wilson, Chadwick Center Director, January 28, 2009.
57   For more information about specific operating costs at model Centers, contact the National Family Justice Center Alliance at www.familyjusticecenter.org.

People and Places
in the FJC Story

Ribbon Cutting for the San Diego Family Justice Center.

Family Justice Center Grand Opening October 10, 2002

Grand Opening Day of the San Diego Family Justice Center—October 10, 2002.

The First Volunteer Academy of the San Diego FJC.

Strategic Planning Meeting for Phase III of the San Diego Family Justice Center.

The San Diego FJC VOICES Committee – Survivors Who Speak Publicly in Support of the Center and Its Work.

Gael Strack and Casey Gwinn.

The National Family Justice Center Alliance Team.
(Picture Courtesy of Sandy Huffaker.)

The New Orleans Family Justice Center Team.

Anaheim Family Justice Center Team.

Ouachita Parish Family Justice Center Team (Monroe, LA).

Bexar County Family Justice Center Team (San Antonio, TX).

The Nampa (ID) FJC Team.

The Hillsborough County FJC Team (Tampa, FL).

*First Middle East Conference on Co-Located Services – November 2009
(Amman, Jordan).*

125

Front porch, Tacoma FJC.

Front Porch, Knoxville FJC.

126

Donor recognition, Nampa FJC.

Brooklyn Family Justice Center – Donor Tree/Grand Opening.

Children's Room, Monterrey, Mexico FJC.

Children's Room, Anaheim FJC. (Sponsored by Disneyland.)

Kitchen, Duluth FJC.

Living Room, Tacoma FJC.

Interview Room – Montgomery County, Maryland FJC.

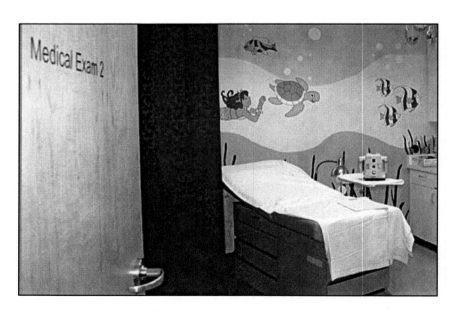

Forensic Room, San Diego.

Computer and Learning Center, Alameda FJC.

Two-way Video with the Courts, Albuquerque FJC.

Coffee Stand, Alameda County FJC.

Large Conference Rooms, Anaheim FJC.

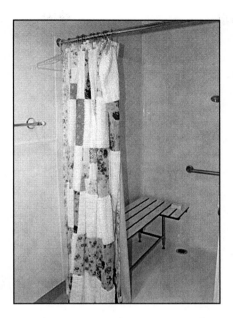

Shower Area, San Diego FJC.

Outdoor Patio, New Orleans FJC.

Lake Superior Regional FJC

Dress for Success Store, Boston FJC.

CHAPTER SIX

When Family Justice Centers Work Well

I want to share the story of a long-term Wellspring client, Christina, who came to see me before we officially opened last year. Christina had married at eighteen years of age to an older, abusive man, and she had two children by him. Lacking education and having low self-esteem, she was not able to remove herself or the children from the abuser. When she did finally leave, Christina entered into another relationship, in which her partner was not violent, but he moved away when his job here ended. It took some time for her to develop the strength to cope with life on her own. She participated in nearly every service the Ouachita Parish FJC offers. Upon her first visit to our Legal Department, she asked only for her legal options. A few weeks after obtaining a protection order, she requested to proceed with a divorce. Due to a prior reconciliation, it was necessary to file a divorce and, under Louisiana law, wait 180 days after he was served with papers to request that the divorce be granted.

Criminal charges were also filed against Christina's husband. Near the time she was subpoenaed to testify in court on the criminal charge of domestic battery, she needed surgery. By the time the court scheduled a Hearing Officer Conference on the issues of custody and child support, she was recovering. The FJC partners visited, called her, and made sure all her court hearings were monitored. Her husband did not attend the Hearing Officer Conference, and she was granted sole custody and child support, all without his protest. When he realized the divorce was imminent, he called me stating she'd lied about it all and that he would fight the divorce and bring witnesses to the 'Show Cause' hearing as to why the court should not grant a divorce. He evaded service of notice of the hearing date for about six weeks. Meanwhile, Christina became homeless when the family member with whom she lived put her out. The Wellspring had to provide housing for her.

Finally, the sheriff managed to serve the abuser with notice of the court's consideration of the finality of the divorce. The client attended the brief hearing with me (her attorney), although she was not required to do so. Her husband did not show up, and the divorce was granted. She is now attending school to learn a trade and has a good place to live. At the end of the court hearing, she stood tall in front of the judge and said, "I am bettering myself and changing my life." It has been a very long time since I've seen such pure happiness shining in someone's eyes as it did in hers.

*Attorney at the Ouachita Parish Family Justice Center
(operated by the Wellspring—a community-based shelter
and domestic violence program)*

There can be little doubt that when everyone works together good things happen for victims of domestic violence and their children. Nearly ten years into the movement towards multi-agency co-located services strong indices of success and effectiveness are beginning to emerge.

RELATIONSHIP BUILDING

Perhaps one of the greatest impacts of attempting to bring everyone together is simply the process of cross-training and relationship building that happens during the journey. The first FJC Director in Ouachita Parish, Louisiana, Tammie Slauson, penned these words soon after they opened their Center:

The Perspective of Former Ouachita Parish FJC Director Tammie Slauson

When the Office on Violence Against Women conducted the site visit in Monroe, Louisiana before awarding us a Family Justice Center grant, one of the judges that was at the meeting told the site visit team, "Five years ago I was a Neanderthal on the issue of domestic violence until these two ladies got a hold of me." He pointed to our Assistant District Attorney and the Domestic Violence Investigator for the Ouachita Parish Sheriff's Department."

This was evidence of the openness, trust level, and dedication of our community's criminal justice system and evidence of the progress we made by simply dreaming together.

The coordination did not happen over night. A multi-disciplinary team began meeting in Ouachita Parish in 1988 to address the issues of domestic violence. In 2002, this same group wrote a Community Response Manual outlining protocols for each discipline responding to domestic violence victims. This effort was enhanced by a massive multi-media campaign targeting key leaders and citizens to make them aware of the devastating effects of domestic violence on our community.

When the Family Justice Center grant opportunity arose in 2004, it was the next logical step. Our team in Ouachita often joked that we had been dating for a while, so it was time to get married and move in together. We did not realize at the time that this metaphor had much validity. Moving in together into a FJC has many of the same joys and struggles as a new marriage. Communication issues arise, conflicts are numerous, and personalities of people and agencies clash, but in the end it is all worth it if you stay committed and focused on helping those that you serve. As with any relationship, success requires focusing on a common goal, building trust and maintaining it, and showing respect and honor for each other.

The journey served a purpose long before the Center was ever ready to become a reality. And the journey is important in laying the groundwork for actually getting married and moving in together!

HOMICIDE REDUCTION

As discussed earlier, many Family Justice Center communities have reported significant drops in domestic violence homicides in the wake of creating or expanding their co-located services models. As discussed in Chapter 5, in New York City, Mayor Michael Bloomberg has taken the lead in launching three regional Family Justice Centers. The Mayor's Office to Combat Domestic Violence coordinates domestic violence services provided by numerous New York City agencies and more than 200 community-based organizations. Since January 2002, Commissioner Yolanda B. Jimenez has worked with the various agencies and organizations to institute a number of new projects and practices, including opening the Brooklyn Family Justice Center in 2005, the Queens Family Justice Center in 2008 and the Bronx Family Justice Center in 2010. The Family Justice Center Initiative is part of the Bloomberg Administration's overall effort to reduce domestic violence and provide comprehensive services to victims. As a result of the City's focus on this issue, family violence related crimes have declined by 21% and intimate partner homicides have declined by 51% citywide.[1] The Mayor widely credits the Family Justice Center collaborative as central to the major crime reductions.

Alameda County has also experienced a dramatic drop in domestic violence homicide from 30 in 2001 to 7 in 2007. The Alameda County Board of Supervisors and the District Attorney's Office has attributed this drop to three major initiatives—the creation of the Alameda County Family Justice Center, the establishment of the Domestic Violence Response Team (DVRT), and the creation of the Sexual Assault Response Teams (SART).[2] This coincided with a notable increase in calls to law enforcement and services provided through shelters, indicators that victims are increasingly seeking help before the violence escalates to homicide in Alameda County. San Diego has also reported major drops in domestic violence homicides since the opening of the San Diego Family Justice Center.

INCREASED PARTICIPATION IN CRIMINAL PROSECUTION BY VICTIMS

One of the biggest challenges facing prosecutors in America today is the ongoing reluctance of victims of family violence to participate in the prosecution of cases against their partners. District Attorney

Nancy O'Malley, however, has documented dramatic improvements in a victim's willingness to testify once the Alameda County Family Justice Center opened in 2006.

In 2006, the first year the Alameda County FJC opened, 55 percent of misdemeanors were not charged because the victim refused to participate and the case was not otherwise provable. In the ensuing three years after the entire prosecution team integrated themselves into the FJC, the percentage of cases that were not charged decreased.

2007: Decreased to 36%
2008: Decreased to 22%
2009: Decreased to 19%

The felony domestic violence cases of the Alameda County District Attorney's Office showed the same pattern. In 2006, 31% of felony domestic violence cases submitted by law enforcement agencies were not charged because the victim refused to participate and the case was not otherwise provable. In the ensuing three years, the percentage of felony cases that were not charged decreased.

2007: Decreased to 23%
2008: Decreased to 18.87%
2009: Decreased to 18.68%

The Nampa Family Justice Center in outcome studies conducted by Boise State University has reported similar impacts. The Croydon Family Justice Centre in the United Kingdom has also reported similar positive impacts on victim willingness to participate in the criminal prosecution process after providing comprehensive services. Indeed, Family Justice Centers in Salt Lake City (UT), San Diego (CA), Anaheim (CA), Tacoma (WA), New York City (NY), Tulsa (OK), and other community have all reported similar feedback from prosecutors and police officers working in their Centers.[3]

The pattern is clear and not surprising. Any domestic violence shelter advocate in America can tell you the same thing. When a victim is wrapped in safety, support and services she does not recant or minimize at nearly the rate she does when she is scared, unsupported, alone, and fully exposed to the threats and manipulation of her abuser.

HIGH LEVELS OF SATISFACTION BY CLIENTS

Multiple evaluations have now been conducted in a variety of Family Justice Centers that demonstrate the positive impacts in the lives of victims seeking services at Centers. In 2008, Boise State University published its Process and Outcome Evaluation of the Nampa Family Justice Center (Nampa, ID). [4]The study evaluated the experience of FJC clients in receiving services and the perceptions of FJC partner agencies in working in a co-located, multi-agency model. Multiple methods of data collection were used to assess the process and short-term effects of the Nampa Family Justice Center (NFJC), which provides multi-agency, co-located services to victims of domestic and dating violence, child abuse, and sexual violence. These methods included (1) the collection of telephone interview data with a sample of agency directors and line-staff from NFJC partner agencies; (2) the utilization of NFJC intake forms to create a baseline client profile; and (3) the creation of a NFJC client exit survey to gauge client satisfaction levels with regard to NFJC staff and services. The evaluation also gauged the effectiveness of services to children (64% had at least one child). The documented findings confirmed high levels of satisfaction from sample of 116 clients. Strikingly, 100% of the clients described an improvement in services received compared to prior contact with the agencies and systems represented in the Center.

> I've never felt this safe in my life and I don't trust often. I felt very comfortable and was strongly supported. Everything and everyone was great. Happy to know that there is help out there.
>
> Alejandra, Albuquerque Family Advocacy Center (2009)
> (Albuquerque, NM)

Recent evaluation funded by Blueshield of California Foundation documented similar satisfaction levels from clients at the San Diego Family Justice Center.[5] A group of 65 clients were randomly identified and agreed to in-depth interviews with Dr. Andrea Hazen or focus group participation. 100% of the clients described strong support for a co-located, multi-agency model and for the services they received.[6] Interestingly, they did have criticism. The criticism they had related to additional services they believed should be on-site and the level of staffing to provide the needed services. The other component of the evaluation involved clients rating themselves before and after FJC services.

Prior to receiving services, 94.74% of the participants reported elevated stress levels in excess of 6 on a 10 scale. After receiving services at the SDFJC, participants with the most heightened stress levels declined to 71.88%. At the time of the focus groups, after receiving additional services and benefiting from the outcome of SDFJC interventions, clients with extremely heightened stress levels declined to 46.43%. By the time of the focus groups, the majority of the clients, 53.57% had reduced stress levels below 5 on a 10 scale. 86.54% of the clients identified positive change in their lives because of services at the FJC. 55.7% described themselves as emotionally stronger because of services they obtained. Notably, this review was done during the challenging period of the Center's history with declining partner agencies and declining client visits. And yet significant positive outcomes were identified in large sample surveys, focus groups, and in-depth interviews.

The clients also vote for the FJC model by coming to it. The Albuquerque Family Advocacy Center has reported that there are now thirteen on-site partner agencies and they are all reporting nearly three times as many clients in each of their agencies as when they were free standing entities serving clients only in their own locations.[7]

The positive client feedback in Centers across the country has been consistent. Victims first say they would like all their services in one place and then they identify those co-located services as beneficial to themselves and their children.

VICTIM-CENTERED INNOVATIONS

Perhaps the most exciting development in the Family Justice Center movement in the last ten years has been the infusion of new energy and creativity around the multi-agency model. New space designs, new program approaches, and new collaborative ideas have emerged that have challenged other Centers to think bigger, to be more creative, and to listen to survivors about they want Centers to look and feel. The more we have asked survivors what they want and what they need the more survivors have helped to design Centers and develop needed programs in Centers.

Front Porches

Most Centers have worked hard to create "front porches" or reception areas that are warm and welcoming. In Knoxville, you feel the Southern hospitality as soon as you walk in the front door. Director Amy Dilworth's heart for her clients is felt the moment they walk in the front door! In New York City (Brooklyn), there is a beautiful donor tree as soon as you arrive that makes you see how many individuals and businesses support the Center. In Alameda County, it is origami art that almost takes your breath away. In Nampa, the coordinated color scheme immediately grabs your attention because of the donation of professional interior design services by a local company. Director Rebecca Lovelace did not want it to feel like a social service agency. She wanted it to send a powerful message of welcome, warmth, and competence from the first moment a client caught a glimpse of the inside of the Center. At the Crystal Judson Family Justice Center in Tacoma, Washington victims daily make comments

> For me this was scary step for a very long time-my welcome here was such that I was compelled to make this move- finally. I'm so glad I have and the staff was very cool!!! I love the calm, peaceful feeling I get from being here. Everyone was very helpful and kind to me. The FJC is very beautifully furnished and has a calm atmosphere.
>
> Anonymous Client, Crystal Judson Family Justice Center
> (Tacoma, WA), 2009

about the facility, the quality, the atmosphere, and the beauty. Such comments are being received in Centers around the country today. For those of us that previously worked out of Police Departments or District Attorney's Offices, we can testify that no one ever complimented our facilities for their warmth, atmosphere, or amenities!

Kitchens and Coffee Areas

In most of the Centers, when a victim arrives with her children she is welcomed into a kitchen area where food is served and the welcome message is delivered loud and clear. In Alameda County, Bosco's Café welcomes clients and makes them feel like they are at a coffee shop instead of a domestic violence center. Named after the former head of their Victim-Witness Assistance Program, Harold Boscovich, the coffee area is one of those little touches that tell a victim she is valuable, respected, and appreciated. Too often victims arrive at Centers scared and tired, with cranky children in tow. The kitchen or dining room area is a place of peace, calm, and fellowship.

Children's Rooms

One of the very special features in many Centers, that has emerged as the movement has evolved is the creation of a special children's room. The vision came from the Child Advocacy Center movement. Former Director of the National Child Advocacy Center in Huntsville, Alabama, Charles Wilson said our goal should be to have rooms where children wanted to have their birthday parties! San Diego gave it a good start, but the Anaheim Family Justice Center set the standard when they had Disneyland design their Children's Room. Wow. And kids do want to have their birthday parties there! How amazing that in a Center where we deal with violence, abuse, trauma, and terror that children love to come there and play while Mom or Dad is seeking services. Many of the rooms are designed so their Moms can be in one place and still see their children playing in the Children's Room—a feature requested in survivor focus groups. So many Centers have created special rooms where children feel welcome and excited to be there—Tacoma, Monterrey (Mexico), Brooklyn, Tampa,

Defiance (OH), San Diego, Duluth, Nampa, and many others have created great rooms for children.

On-Site Salon

The Lake Superior Family Justice Center (Duluth) gets the prize for best salon in a Center. Building on the national "Cut it Out" campaign, Duluth partnered with a local salon to have a beautiful little salon room. Instead of the client having to go to a local salon for a makeover, the local stylist comes to the Family Justice Center to provide that special service. Another way to reject "referrals" and another way to make it easier for a victim to receive all needed services in one place!

Dress for Success

A number of Centers have reached out to their local Dress for Success chapter to bring their program inside the Family Justice Center. The Boston Family Justice Center led the way, with the strong support of Joi Gordon, the President and CEO of Dress for Success. They set up a beautiful boutique right inside the Center—again rejecting a "referral" approach and providing the services of Dress for Success right in the Center.

Electronic Safety Deposit Boxes

The Verizon Foundation has helped fund one of the newest services coming to Family Justice Centers—called the electronic safety deposit box. Designed with survivor input and counsel from the Safety Net Team of the National Network to End Domestic Violence, the project helps victims scan all their documents and store them on a password-protected flash drive or on a confidential Internet account. The National Family Justice Center Alliance has developed the project through pilot testing at Family Justice Centers in Nampa, New Orleans, Tampa, and San Diego. Once the protocols are finalized and victim input is received on the beneficial components of the program, the electronic safety deposit box can be made available to victims of domestic violence across the United States. Too often we see the victim with hundreds of pages of legal papers, medical records, police reports, and a host of other documents stuffed into her diaper bag when she arrives at our agencies. Yet, no one has offered to organize them, scan them, and store them in a safe, confidential, simple, easy way for her. The collaboration between Verizon, survivors, and the FJC Alliance has produced an innovative approach to this pressing need.

> Our first E-Box client had fifteen pounds of documents she needed scanned onto a flash drive. She was carrying them everywhere she went because she was afraid her abuser would find them and steal them. It was every medical record, every police report, her birth certificate, her bank records, her court documents, and a host of other papers. When we told her we could scan them all, organize them into file folders, and put them on a password-protected flash drive, you would have thought we have just offered her a million dollars. It took nearly five hours to go through everything with her, but when we were done and I handed her a little thumb drive with everything on it, she beaming from ear to ear. The look of relief on her face was worth the tedious hours it took to get everything scanned.
>
> Brenda Lugo
> FJC Legal Network
> San Diego Family Justice Center

Support, Support, Support

When agencies come together in one place, the support system for a victim increases exponentially. In many Centers, the support is no longer one advocate from one agency. The support team may include volunteers at a Center, a detective, a prosecutor, a nurse, a doctor, a counselor, a child trauma specialist, a locksmith, a civil attorney, a court support advocate, and many others. Over and over victims say they feel like everyone is on their side at Family Justice Centers. They are overwhelmed by how many people are all trying to protect them, advocate for them, and help them. It is not the same dynamic when a victim must travel from place to place and agency to agency seeking the services she or he needs.

I had a marvelous detective (Greg Olsen) and a counselor from the Center for Community Solutions. They got me through the devastation and the physical injuries. They were a godsend for communicating with the DA and everyone, especially after my phone was shut off. With my father with Alzheimer's and a number of deaths in the family, I was able to come to the Family Justice Center to get assistance, take a deep breath, have tea, and get help. Almost daily, I commuted 30 miles from Oceanside, used the phone here, used the Internet, and met with anyone who would help and see me. I was here so often it was my second home.

Anonymous Family Justice Center Client, 2004

Accessible, Holistic Legal Services

One of the great innovations of Family Justice Centers has been accessible legal assistance without having to go to court. The Tulsa Family Safety Center led the way with a video hook-up to Family Court for its clients. Director Kate Reeves has a tremendous background in fundraising and non-profit leadership and she is applying that expertise in Tulsa to keep developing their legal services model to be more effective, more holistic, and more responsive to a victim's needs. The Anaheim FJC has followed their lead working closely with the Superior Court and Chapman University School of Law. Police Chief John Welter has leveraged his connections and relationships, in a police-led Center, to reach out to the civil legal community to do things that police departments don't usually spend their time doing. But victims are the beneficiaries of his willingness to think outside the box.

Other Centers are using fax or electronic filing protocols to allow victims to file for restraining orders without having to go to court. While the children play at the FJC, Mom or Dad are in another room working with a lawyer and filing their application for legal protection without ever leaving the Family Justice Center! Social services can be delivered at the same time and in the same place as civil legal services. With coordination with police departments and prosecutors' offices, it is also easier to get police reports and copies of evidence in the criminal case if everyone is co-located. Easier access to the evidence produces better applications for restraining orders and better evidence when judges consider issuing long-term, permanent court orders of protection. If there is an on-site Forensic Medical Unit, pictures can be taken at the same time that the civil legal team is preparing the restraining order application. The pictures can then be easily attached and the judge's job in court becomes so much easier.

This innovation was not previously reported in any domestic violence shelter in America prior to the first protocol created for the San Diego Family Justice Center. After San Diego began this protocol with the San Diego Superior Court, the San Diego Domestic Violence Council successfully advocated for the application of this protocol to the Legal Clinic at the YWCA of San Diego County. To date, no other program besides the San Diego Family Justice Center and the YWCA have access to this victim-friendly service.

The Crystal Judson Family Justice Center in Tacoma has taken the use of technology one step further with their new Kiosk Program. Susan Adams and Craig Roberts who provide leadership in Tacoma have refused to simply get the Center operational. They are regularly asking: What else can be done? What else can be tried? What else do victims need? The Kiosk Program is one of those innovations that started before the FJC but has now been dramatically expanded and enhanced because of the FJC.

Medical Services

Another innovation in Family Justice Centers has been the placement of health clinics or Forensic Medical Units right on site. Domestic violence shelters long ago realized the benefit of medical services on site for victims and their children. In the FJC model, this also produces better evidence for civil and criminal cases. Albuquerque (NM) has set the standard at their Center by bringing in their sexual assault examination process right at the Center. Because of Joanne Fine's vision, victims of sexual assault don't have to go to a hospital or off-site location. They can receive social services, victim assistance, and medical services all in one place. The new Valley Cares Family Justice Center in Los Angeles is combining domestic violence services with their sexual assault response team and will have that same powerful combi-

Crystal Judson Family Justice Center Kiosk Program

Electronically filed protection orders were first piloted in Pierce County in Gig Harbor, Washington, beginning in January, 2004. The second phase of the project was implemented in April, 2004, in Lakewood, WA. Electronically filed protection orders have proved to be an asset to our community. This project has increased access to protection orders for victims, simplified the petition process, increased domestic violence awareness in our community, and forged new partnerships in the community.

The kiosk project enables victims to file for temporary protection orders within their own communities instead of driving to the county court house, which can be up to a two hour drive for many residents in our county. The kiosks are located in secure locations within civic buildings, allowing easy access and having ample parking for petitioners. The kiosks are located in safe, quiet areas with staff available to assist petitioners. When the Crystal Judson Family Justice Center opened in 2005, there were two kiosks for clients to use to file protection orders. Due to demand, there are now ten kiosks!

The computers have simplified the filing process for a protection order. The computers have made this process quicker and easier for petitioners. Before the computers were used to file for protection orders, petitioners had to complete several pages of paperwork by hand writing them, a process which could take over an hour. Much of the information had to be written a number of times on the cumbersome forms. The computer is quicker and it automatically duplicates information needed on different pages, and highlights in red when a petitioner has missed some pertinent information on a screen. The petitioner cannot proceed to the next screen until all required fields have been completed. Each screen also has helpful tips for filling out the petition. These tips alleviate the need to stop the process and ask for help.

Each kiosk start-up, many of which the FJC has facilitated under an Encourage Arrest Grant, has been an opportunity for a "grand opening" where local officials presided and local media were present. This kiosk grand opening created a forum not only to inform the public about the kiosk, but also about domestic violence issues.

nation of services in one place thanks to the financial investment and leadership of Mike Wall, the CEO of Northridge Hospital.

Chaplain's Programs

Family Justice Centers have also facilitated a discussion on how best to provide spiritual care services to victims of domestic violence. The vision first started in San Diego when Dr. Mickey Stonier, a local pastor and Fire Department Chaplain challenged us to understand that spiritual care is one of the greatest needs of trauma victims whether the trauma is from a natural disaster, a terror attack, or domestic violence. We quickly found that if victims were offered the support of a chaplain, they would take it. The traditional approach in DV organizations to "refer" victims to their own faith community was not meeting the need. Rev. David Kitts, in Knoxville (TN), has really helped us move the vision forward. He has helped us understand that victims may often be getting "referred" back to a pastor, priest, or rabbi who knows nothing about domestic violence. Her abuser is likely in the same church or parish. And she may already be facing victim blaming from her spiritual leader because she is "not a good enough wife" or "does not respect her husband" or is unwilling to "submit" to his leadership in her life.

Spiritual care, like other FJC services, should not be a referral. It should be available onsite. If it is, victims will access those services and it will be transformative. Rev. Mike Neely in Tampa, Florida has seen the power of providing chaplaincy to victims at the Center and he has also seen the benefit to his own congregation. Rev. Neely started volunteering at the Hillsborough County Family Justice Center and built a close working relationship with the Director, Nikki Daniels. Then, the roof blew off his church building and his church had no place to meet. Nikki made the FJC available on Sundays since no one was using it. As soon as Mike's church was meeting at the FJC, they started to learn more about domestic violence. They were there every week! They saw the needs and started volunteering. Women and men heard more about domestic violence and had to deal with issues in their own lives. And Mike saw that sometimes losing the roof of your church can lead to powerful, positive ministry in the lives of hurting people!

Art, Music, Animals, and Recreation

Many shelters and community-based domestic violence agencies have realized the power of music, art, animal therapy, and recreation in the lives of victims of abuse and their children. An FJC-type shelter, the Julian Center, in Indianapolis, first showed us what can be done. The Julian Center uses broken glass and tumbled porcelain with their clients and children to create beautiful mosaics that hang in the Center and can be sold to raise funds for their programs. Family Justice Centers have been late to this party but slowly Centers are starting to realize the importance of these mediums to touch lives. Recently, San Diego has partnered with the Rainforest Project to create a unique approach to art that has tremendous promise for the future.[8] The FJC partnered with the YWCA and the Avon Foundation to create a ten week art class for women and children to create a traveling exhibit of tumbled glass. The Rainforest Project is led by Dan Evers and Yesenia Aceves, two gifted artists who have a heart for hurting families and abused children. In consultation with the FJC, Dan and Yesenia chose butterflies for the theme and had a former FJC client and YWCA client design the mosaic. The class is not officially "art therapy", it is art for the sake of beauty and expression. But in the process healing happens, joy emerges, and laughter bounces of the walls. The Rainforest Project has promise for Centers across the country as a way to welcome clients long after the crisis and a way to offer hope and healing.

San Diego also led the way in promoting camping and mentoring as a long-term prevention component of the FJC model. Camp HOPE has been a very special part of the San Diego FJC vision and other Centers are now pursuing camping opportunities for children and women exposed to domestic violence. Camping professionals and mentoring programs can become excellent partners in many Family Justice Centers across the country in years to come. As we write, Camp HOPE is struggling to maintain its funding but for seven years, hundreds of the FJC children have come to camp and benefited from getting out of their home environment and being able to be kids in a monitored, safe, structured camping environment where they can kayak, canoe, fish, water ski, wakeboard, tube, roast s'mores, sing by a campfire, and look up at the stars.

Animals too have proven to be powerful allies to battered women and abused children. Animal therapy is being used in many domestic violence shelters and the power of the approach works in Family Justice Centers. Just days before writing this chapter, an FJC client in San Diego testified in court in a domestic violence case with a yellow lab at her side! She met the dog during her medical exam in the Forensic Medical Unit at the Center and he quickly became a comforting friend, ally, and advocate! Weeks later she was so terrified to testify against her husband that she asked if the dog could be in court. The judge authorized it and she testified with confidence even while stroking the hair of her four legged advocate in front of the jury!

Self-Sufficiency Coordinators

One of the new focus areas of the FJC movement is the area of job training and job placement. Many domestic violence programs seek to promote this focus area by helping victims with resume preparation, interview training, or referrals to job training programs. Family Justice Centers and community-based programs that have a partnering approach can also bring other agencies in to do this for their clients on site. The focus on helping victims manage their money, know what public benefits they are eligible for, and plan for their future is a critical one.

In the Brooklyn Family Justice Center, Director Jennifer DeCarli has helped promote a new position called the Self-Sufficiency Coordinator. It is one of the many services that victims need after the crisis intervention effort is over. How do they get public benefits? How much can they get? How do they coordinate this with the effort to get child support? How much can they make and still receive food stamps? Portions of the job are social work 101 but other pieces involve the coordination of everything that is going on in the life of the victim—it is part case management, part advocate, part friend, part financial planner, and part job training and job placement assistance! In Alameda County, they are developing a somewhat similar position called a "Navigator" to help the victim navigate the system and the many issues that she must address in the journey to self-sufficiency and safety. Integrating public benefits and public assistance into the "under one roof" FJC model is another excellent area for future innovation. There are numerous model programs now for empowerment around the country in FJCs.

We dream of a day when Family Justice Centers and other kinds of multi-agency service delivery models have all the assistance related to self-sufficiency right at the Center where the victim comes for services. As the victim is welcomed into the FJC community, she or he can keep coming back to a community that cares and has the services and partner agencies there to provide the help that is needed.

Cultural Competency

Family Justice Centers often shine in the arena of cultural competency and diversity by bringing together diverse community partner agencies that represent the diversity of a community. Every community has agencies and communities that represent their diversity. The problem is that many non-profits don't have that kind of diversity within their own staff and their own focus areas. But when you bring in multiple agencies representing all disciplines and all cultural and ethnic groups within a community you begin to have a collaborative that represents the entire community. While processes and procedures are still necessary to build respect, communication, and partnership among such diverse partners, there is a solid foundation when the collaborative represents the diversity of the entire community.

New York City has set the standard in this arena and Mayor Michael Bloomberg deserves recognition for his visionary leadership. Few cities in the United States have the diversity and cultural complexity evidenced in New York City. Language groups, ethnic groups, socio-economic groups, and racial groups abound. New York City is one of the most cosmopolitan and diverse cities on the planet. And yet, the Mayor has created a series of Family Justice Centers that have helped to reflect this diversity and in the process has created acces-

Recognizing the Work of Powerful Visionaries in New York City

In July 2004, the Mayor's Office to Combat Domestic Violence (OCDV) with lead partner agency, the Kings County District Attorney's Office (KCDA), was awarded a $1.2 million grant from the Department of Justice (DOJ) Office on Violence Against Women (OVW), to launch a Family Justice Center in Brooklyn (BKFJC). Mayor Michael R. Bloomberg opened the BKFJC in July 2005 to provide a facility for essential advocacy, case management, and criminal and civil legal assistance for domestic violence victims and their children all under one roof. The BKFJC has marshaled the expertise of 19 on-site organizations including City and State agencies, and non-profit organizations, to provide clients with the most reliable, culturally competent, and comprehensive services available. With both public and private resources, the BKFJC helps domestic violence victims break the cycle of violence by streamlining the process of receiving services. Since its opening in July 2005 through March 2010, the BKFJC has served over 30,000 unique clients and there have been over 62,000 client visits. The BKFJC is currently averaging 1,700 client visits each month. Based on the success of the City's first Center in Brooklyn, and the City's commitment to providing comprehensive services for victims of domestic violence, Mayor Bloomberg along with OCDV Commissioner Yolanda B. Jimenez opened a Queens Center in July 2008 and a third Center in the Bronx is scheduled to open in 2010.

In addition to providing clients with immediate crisis intervention and services, OCDV has ensured that the City's Centers have become a place to which clients return for other important long-term services. For example, the Centers each have a self-sufficiency program which focuses on addressing the multiple needs confronting domestic violence victims escaping abusive relationships. These needs include assistance with affordable housing and public assistance, English as a Second Language Classes, financial literacy classes, high school equivalency classes, scholarship application assistance, and managed referrals for job training, education and employment. Most recently, the Centers also launched a nine week bilingual (English and Spanish) Family Literacy Program for children and caregivers, supported by private funding.

At the New York City Family Justice Centers, key client documents have been translated into the top seven languages spoken at the Centers and by mid-2010, will be available in 16 languages. In addition, the Centers partner with on-site partner agencies that specialize in working with specific cultural groups, such as the Arabic, the Asian, Latina, the Russian and

Caribbean populations and there is a City-funded, full-time immigration attorney located on-site at each of the Centers. Further, all partner staff members are required to take cultural competency and language access training and utilize language line interpretation services. This commitment by New York City to ensure access to critically important services for all victims of domestic violence, regardless of their language or immigration status, is a key component to the success of the New York City Family Justice Centers.

sibility and effective service delivery. The self-sufficiency coordinator positions and their language accessibility both support their vision.

THE FJC IS COORDINATED COMMUNITY RESPONSE ON STEROIDS

In 2008, Ellen Pence spoke at the International Family Justice Center Conference in San Diego, CA and she placed Family Justice Centers onto the continuum of service delivery models and community responses to family violence: "The Family Justice Center movement is coordinated community response on steroids!"[9] Five hundred attendees laughed and enjoyed the image in the crazy, mad era of steroid use in professional sports but Ellen was right. Communities that have developed a coordinated community response have laid the groundwork for having Family Justice Centers. And with the foundation laid, the power of the co-located, multi-agency model is magnified in expanding the influence and impact of strong, close working relationships among individuals and agencies.

Coordinated community responses to family violence have been identified as a best practice in the field of family violence prevention and intervention.[10] Coordinated community response is an intervention strategy promulgated by the Domestic Abuse Intervention Project (DAIP) in the small city of Duluth and later developed and promoted in metropolitan cities like San Diego and communities across the United States. Coordinated community response is a "system of networks, agreements, processes and applied principles created by the local shelter movement, criminal justice agencies, and human service programs that were developed in a small northern

Minnesota city over a fifteen year period. It is still a project in the making." [11]

DAIP found that when different members of the community coordinated their efforts to protect battered women and hold batterers accountable, these efforts were more successful. Coordination helps to ensure that the system works faster and better for victims, that victims are protected and receive the services they need, and that batterers are held accountable and cease their abusive behavior.

Law enforcement agencies, advocates, health care providers, child protection services, local businesses, the media, employers, faith communities, and others working with victims of domestic violence should be involved in a coordinated community response. Health care providers are often critical participants. Doctors, nurses, and emergency room workers may see and treat women who do not or cannot seek other kinds of assistance. The goal of a coordinated community response is to create an accessible network of support for victims and their families.

Coordination of the responses of those in the community who come into contact with domestic violence issues has significantly increased victim protection and batterer accountability in many communities. Coordination that is based on increased victim safety has been identified to be beneficial in four different ways. First, the effectiveness of many responses depends on the effectiveness of others. Second, different actors may encounter victims at different points and in different settings. Each has opportunities others may not have to help victims locate the resources they may need. Third, recruiting the general public to ask for their help in a coordinated community response can increase the effectiveness of the response. Fourth, a comprehensive community response can address related social problems that work to prevent women from gaining protection. Emergency shelter and criminal prosecutions are not the only needs that battered women may have. Coordinated response programs are increasingly focused on related social problems that make it difficult for women to seek protection from abuse, such as poverty and unemployment or the lack of affordable housing.[12]

The Family Justice Center model, by co-locating all the partners or many of the partners in a coordinated community response model, can magnify the benefits of such coordination while making it easier for victims to obtain the services they need.

THE GREENBOOK INITIATIVE POINTED TOWARD MULTI-AGENCY CO-LOCATED MODELS

It is not only clients that confirm the importance of the model. The co-located services model was also recommended in The Greenbook Initiative, the largest federal evaluation of systems issues surrounding the co-occurrence of child abuse and domestic violence ever sponsored by the United States Department of Justice.[13] The Greenbook Initiative, the Child Advocacy Center movement, and even the Federal Emergency Management Agency have advocated for the use of co-located services to more easily meet the needs of victims of trauma and abuse. It is extremely logical. People who have experienced severe trauma need to be able to come one place for services instead of having to navigate complicated systems while dealing with major emotional, physical, and mental challenges.

> Co-location of services is one of the recommendations in the Greenbook. The newly developing Family Justice Centers can demonstrate that there are hurdles, of course, but there are also benefits. One of the major barriers for families getting help is the fragmentation among and lack of knowledge about the services available. The FJC partnership model is resource efficient. Some form of an FJC would be great in every community.
>
> Dr. Jeff Edelson, Director of the Minn. Center Against Violence and Abuse
> Co-Author of the Greenbook Initiative Report

The Greenbook Initiative applied coordinated community response principles to the complex interactions between the courts, child welfare agencies, and domestic violence agencies. So, it makes sense that the concept of multi-agency, co-located services was a key focus area at the conclusion of the Initiative. Many of the Greenbook sites have struggled to make this recommendation a reality but the need was clear.

Family Justice Centers are leading the way in model programs to address the co-occurrence of domestic violence and child abuse. They are doing what the Greenbook recommended even though many of the Greenbook sites themselves have struggled to co-locate critical services to address the very issues that the Initiative identified.

Two programs are worthy of particular mention though many Centers have done an excellent job of bringing in partner agencies and allied organizations to meet the needs of victims of domestic violence who have children that have been exposed to domestic violence. The Stepping Stones Program at the Crystal Judson Family Justice Center in Tacoma, Washington and the Joe Torre Safe at Home Foundation in the Brooklyn and Queens Family Justice Centers in New York City.

Joe Torre Safe at Home Foundation—Brooklyn and Queens Family Justice Centers (NYC)

The Joe Torre Safe at Home Foundation has been one of the City's key partners in the NYC Family Justice Centers. The foundation has funded the children's room named 'Margaret's Place' and the parent and children's counseling program located in both at the Brooklyn Center and now in Queens. More than 3,000 children who have come to the Brooklyn Center, visited Margaret's Place, and met with an advocate. In addition, since November 2006, 33% of the children who have been assessed have begun one-on-one and/or group counseling.

Family Justice Center communities are turning this recommendation into a reality whether they bring child welfare professionals into their Centers or co-locate with them. In Nampa (ID), the Family Justice Center has become a certified Child Advocacy Center to ensure that women are getting the protection and support they need in the process of dealing with co-occurring child abuse. In Ouachita Parish (LA), the Family Justice Center and the Child Advocacy Center have set up operations in buildings right next to each other. In San Diego (CA), the Chadwick Center has co-located their child trauma therapists at the Family Justice Center and have cross-trained them

Stepping Stones at the Crystal Judson Family Justice Center (Tacoma, WA)

Stepping Stones is an 8-week series of classes for mothers and their children ages 6-11. Stepping Stones is an educational family intervention program designed to address the impact of domestic violence on children and the non-offending parent. The goal of the Stepping Stones program is to strengthen the family's ability to deal with the impact of domestic violence. It also provides a powerful venue with parents to talk with their children about the violence they have witnessed. Clients at the FJC are praising Stepping Stones as a powerful venue to talk and crucial to the healing of their children.

in domestic violence advocacy services. In South Bend (IND), the Family Justice Center and the Child Advocacy Center are only blocks apart from each other and have developed tremendous collaborative and interactive relationships. Many other Centers are also developing model protocols for collaboration and interaction around a fundamental FJC principle—**You cannot protect children if you do not protect their mothers.** The Family Justice Center movement has become a laboratory to apply the Greenbook Initiative recommendations and findings and keep moving us forward in dealing with the co-occurrence of child abuse and domestic violence.

...We've all got to join together and start persuading America that unless we invest in community initiatives that look at the family and the child as a whole, we will never be able to build enough prisons 18 years from now....

Hon. Janet Reno
Former U.S. Attorney General

CONCLUSION

When Family Justice Centers work well, good things happen for victims of domestic violence. When victim safety stays front and center, when Centers stay accountable to their clients, co-located services become a powerful, effective way to help hurting families. Well-run

Centers tend to lead to homicide reductions, higher levels of accountability for abusers, high levels of satisfaction from survivors, better innovation, and more effective coordinated community response. So... what happens when Centers don't run well? What happens with the wrong leader? What happens if the local shelter is not included or if they choose not to join the collaborative effort with civil and criminal justice professionals? What happens when agencies never should have moved in together or they move in together and things go wrong? Read on...

NOTES

1　　See http://www.webhse.com/pdfs/2008.07.18-01_nyc_queens.pdf

2　　See www.familyjusticecenter.org/ResourceLibrary for a copy of the Alameda County FJC 2008 Report

3　　These impacts should not be surprising. Victim-witness programs in prosecutor's offices across the United States were developed based on clear evidence that stronger support for victims and witnesses of crime would make it easier for them to participate in the prosecution of criminal offenders.

4　　See www.familyjusticecenter.org/ResourceLibrary for a copy of the Boise State University Study.

5　　For a copy of the Final Evaluation Report, contact the National Family Justice Center Alliance at (888) 511-3522.

6　　Id. The research was conducted during a time of major upheaval in the Center with partners leaving, long waits for services, and many agencies not offering assistance to walk-in clients because of low staff levels and very few volunteers. Yet, the feedback from clients still overwhelmingly endorsed the co-located service model. There was actually no negative feedback except the concern about the role of child welfare services. This issue has now been addressed as it must be in every Center to ensure that victims are receiving the advocacy and support they need in order to be able to maintain custody of their children and enhance the accountability of the abuser for the violence and abuse that have been experienced by mother and child.

7　　See Albuquerque Family Advocacy Center Statistical Report—November 2009, p. 1. To request a copy of the report go to: http://www.cabq.gov/police/fac/index.html.

8　　See www.mychildsrainforest.org for more information about this exciting new project.

9　　Keynote Presentation of Ellen Pence, April 23, 2008, International FJC Conference, San Diego, CA

10　San Diego has been profiled in numerous coordinated community response reviews. To view one of the first reviews of five cities in America, go to: http://aspe.hhs.gov/hsp/cyp/DOMVILNZ.HTM.

11　Ellen Pence & Martha McMahon, A Coordinated Community Response to Domestic Violence, The National Training Project, Duluth, Minnesota.

12　See Ellen L. Pence, Some Thoughts on Philosophy, in Coordinating Community Responses to Domestic Violence: Lessons from the Duluth Model 25, 33 (Melanie F. Shepard & Ellen L. Pence eds., 1999).

13　See www.thegreenbook.info for more information on the Initiative and the current work of the Obama Administration around this critical focus area for the domestic violence movement.

CHAPTER SEVEN

Leadership Matters

Yvonne moved in with Mitch six months after they met in a karate class. She worked in a photography store. He was a former teacher, now a law student. He had teenage children and was a single father after his wife had died from cancer. He was winsome and physically fit, and quickly fell madly in love with Yvonne as soon as they met. His constant attention, notes, phone calls, flowers, and compliments overwhelmed her within weeks of their decision to get involved with each other. But she did, in her heart of hearts, enjoy all the attention. They bonded quickly and when he asked her to move in, it seemed to make sense. Within weeks of giving up her apartment, she saw his rage for the first time. It was over something stupid. But his rage was consuming and terrifying. Within days, the rage turned physical. Yvonne called the police the first time Mitch hit her. She soon realized she must leave him. He was a dangerous man. Though some personal contact continued as she slowly extricated her life from his, she knew that it would never be a healthy relationship. By then, however, she had developed a close relationship with both his daughters. They still worked out at the same karate studio. And they had quickly developed mutual friends.

Police took a report of Mitch's first physical abuse, but he successfully convinced Yvonne that he would leave her alone if she would not press charges. She feared his legal training and did not want to have to face him in court. She never recanted her statement, but she did not return the domestic violence detective's phone calls.

Within days of promising to leave her alone, though, Mitch started calling her, writing her notes, and begging to get back together. Yvonne did everything she was supposed to do. She called the Volunteer Lawyer Program and soon obtained a restraining order. Each time Mitch contacted her, she called the police. She kept a journal and contacted a private lawyer. In a four-month period, Yvonne ended up dealing with more than 10 agencies and individuals in the criminal and civil justice systems as she tried to get help. She was forced to tell her story over and over again. She was referred from one agency to another.

Incidents happened in multiple jurisdictions, and different agencies referred her to other agencies. As she sank into depression from the constant harassment, the bewildering system she was supposed to seek help from became a confusing blur of jurisdictional lines, differing policies and procedures, and multiple locations. She met with the District Attorney's stalking team but was later referred to the City Attorney's Office. She almost lost her job and finally had to contact a private therapist for help.

I met Yvonne after the case was forwarded as a simple restraining order violation to the San Diego City Attorney's Office. Though I was serving as the elected City Attorney, I had taken six weeks out of my regular job that summer to handle a caseload in our specialized Domestic Violence Unit. Sitting in a little office in the middle of the 35-member prosecution unit, I read the police report, which described an incident in which Mitch had been found lying on the front seat of his car around the corner from Yvonne's job. She called the police, believing she had seen him watching her. As officers approached the car, Mitch pretended to be asleep. After they asked him to step out of the car, he told them he dropped off his daughter at her school nearby and then got sleepy while driving home and parked the car. The officers informed him he was less than 1,000 yards from Yvonne's employment location, and though not technically within 300 yards of her person, his behavior was harassing and menacing. Mitch told the officers Yvonne should not be afraid of him. He said if he really wanted to kill her, he would use one of his high-powered rifles and shoot her from a long distance. He said if he was really stalking her, she would never know he was there.

After two interviews with Yvonne, we pieced together the long history of stalking in the relationship. We identified over 60 illegal contacts Mitch had made, contacted the 10 agencies that had been involved, and identified a host of witnesses who had valuable information about Mitch's harassing behavior. We arrested Mitch on the day of his last final in his last year of law school on a $500,000 bench warrant. Later that day, we seized 11 of Mitch's firearms from his father's house, including automatic handguns and a number of rifles with high-powered scopes. Finally, we pulled all the pieces together and started connecting all the agencies that had been involved with this couple in order to hold an abuser accountable and provide safety and support to an extremely traumatized victim of violence and stalking.

Mitch and Yvonne's case played itself out two years before the opening of the San Diego Family Justice Center. It became powerful encouragement for collaboration between agencies, even in a case with a happy ending. Although more than 10 agencies had been involved, none knew what the other agencies were doing. Agency personnel never met together to work on the case. The agencies never sent staff to one place for Yvonne's benefit. Yvonne had to go from place to place in the middle of shock, trauma, and fear to try to get help. Her effort to get agencies to pay attention to her took nearly a year. Thankfully, she did not give up or die during that terrifying 12-month period!

Yvonne is one of my heroes. Today, she works in a Family Justice Center as a Court Support Advocate. And no one is more passionate about the need for coordinated co-located services than Yvonne. She lived and breathed a disjointed system and now she is a powerful voice for creating Family Justice Centers. She also saw that one person, acting as a leader/case manager/coordinator/advocate could make an enormous difference.

Trying to coordinate all the agencies that Yvonne needed help from, seeing how I could make a difference by using the power of my position and my relationships with many different agencies was probably one of my earliest lessons about the power of leadership in collaborative models. As the Family Justice Center movement has evolved though we have seen the importance of leadership much more directly. Coordinating councils have hired the wrong leaders, co-located service models have ended up with the wrong agency in the lead, and Family Justice Centers have hired the wrong Director. And with each example that we have witnessed or that has been brought to our attention, we have gained wisdom about the critical nature of leadership

This first of two chapters about challenges and issues in Family Justice Centers and co-located service models rightly focuses on the issue of leadership. The Advisory Board of the National Family Justice Center Alliance has identified leadership as one of the most pressing issues in the collaborative service delivery model of the Family Justice Center. Today, there are more than sixty operating Centers and nearly one hundred Centers in some stage of planning. Major positive outcomes have been identified in research in New York City, Oakland (CA), San Diego (CA), Nampa (ID), and other Centers as we have discussed earlier in this book. But the truth must be spoken…no matter how good a plan, no matter how dedicated the people involved, no matter how dynamic a Center might be at one point in time…one person can screw it all up.

LEADERSHIP MATTERS

Glen Aubrey in his new book on Abraham Lincoln and the path to effective leadership said of Lincoln, "He could speak to them because he was one of them."[1] Aubrey goes on to point out how Lincoln connected with those that followed him. He understood their issues, he spoke their language, and he listened to their concerns. Phil Eastman in his new book, "The Character of Leadership: An Ancient Model for a Quantum Age," focuses on the inextricable links between relationships and leadership.[2] Eastman makes the point that the most effective leadership is not "top-down" or "telling people what to do." The most effective leadership happens when the leader wins the hearts of those they wish to lead toward a vision or a set of goals.[3]

These fundamental principles have never been better illustrated than in Family Justice Centers. Some Centers have picked the wrong leader right from the start and have suffered major consequences until they found the right leader. Others had a good leader but did not engage in an appropriate succession planning process and ended up with the wrong second leader. Yet others have picked a leader who came from a "chain of command" organization and then tried to order partner agencies to do what they wanted at a Center with disastrous results. Family Justice Centers are not bureaucracies and are not structured to function well under a top-down or chain of command power structure. The many agencies that might have staff in a Center still have their own management structures. Their employees may work at a Center but they must answer to their supervisors within their own organizational structure. Everyone is coming together in one place but they don't work for the Director of the Center where they are co-locating. It is, in the truest sense, collaboration. And there is now a body of literature and there are great examples of how collaborative leadership works best in a Family Justice Center.

COLLABORATIVE LEADERSHIP IS AN ART FORM

Madeleine Carter, writing for the Center for Effective Public Policy as part of a research project funded by the United States Department of Justice and the State Justice Institute, has defined the five qualities of a collaborative leader:

- Willingness to take risks

- Eager listener

- Passion for the cause

- Optimistic about the future

- Able to share power and credit.[4]

Each of these qualities is critical to success for a Family Justice Center leader. First, an FJC Director must be willing to take risks.

This means a willingness to try new approaches, trust others to do their work without being micromanaged, and a desire to constantly improve the way things are being done. Second, an FJC Director must be a good listener. Listening is critical in interacting with survivors, partner agencies, and even detractors. Being willing to accept criticism and then constructively apply that criticism in order to be responsive to the concerns expressed is important if a Center is going to be accountable to survivors and responsive to the needs they express. Third, a Director must have a passion for the cause. Some Centers have made the mistake of hiring a Director with no background in domestic violence and no real passion for the cause. This has generally ended badly. Many who work in the field have a strong passion for the work. They are motivated by like-minded leaders. If they have a leader that does not share their passion, they rarely respond to such a leader.

Fourth, a Director needs to be a positive person with a forward looking approach. There is nothing worse than a negative leader in a collaborative service delivery model. The negativity of the leader will spread like a cancer among the partners in the collaborative. Positive people generally attract positive people and help positive people stay positive! Negative people generally attract negative people and cause positive people to get more negative! Finally, FJC Directors that shine brightly are able to share power and credit. During her five years leading the San Diego FJC, Gael was a master at sharing power and sharing credit. Partner agencies loved her for it and they recognized her as their Director even though most of them did not work for her. Across the board, when Centers have a Director who does not share power or wants all the credit and glory, things go badly. When they brag about their partners, profile them regularly, and let them participate in major decisions, the partners feel invested, loyal, and motivated to improve the work of the Center.

When Gael and I first started working on an FJC Director Toolkit that has now become a resource for all Family Justice Centers in selecting a first Director and hiring subsequent Directors, we made the job description and then studied it for a few minutes, looked at each other, and burst out laughing. Neither one of us was qualified enough to run a Center! We wanted a lawyer, a cop, a social worker, a gifted public speaker, an accountant, and a visionary leader all in one! The complexity of bringing together 15—25 agencies, coordinating different personalities, different value systems, different work cultures was overwhelming enough. But then throwing in the skills necessary to manage a budget, coordinate day to day activities, raise money, develop an outreach effort, and address conflicts and crises on a day to basis…we laughed at promoting a movement and calling for gifted leaders with a job description that perhaps only a handful of people on the planet could be fully qualified to fill! And yet, it can be done, it has been done, and gifted leaders are being identified regularly to lead such co-located Centers across the United States and around the world.

When the work is done well, it can also help communities do both intervention and prevention work in dealing with family violence. Too often, when we focus on family violence we don't realize that by making family violence more of a public safety issue we can draw far more attention to the issue and draw more resources. One visionary leader that deserves recognition for such an approach is Anaheim (CA) Chief of Police John Welter. Chief Welter was the visionary behind the Center just miles from Disneyland and his passion for prevention should motivate many others in law enforcement to follow his lead as they pursue the co-located services vision.

LEADERS NEED TO APPLY THE GUIDING PRINCIPLES

The National Family Justice Center Alliance and its national advisory board have created a set of ten guiding principles that come from the heart of the battered women's movement in the United States and help frame the values that successful leaders must embrace. The guiding principles have been affirmed by most operating Centers, by leaders in the national domestic violence movement, and by survivors of domestic violence who have provided insight and input in their

> Family Justice Centers have the potential to transform the way many communities help victims of domestic violence. They also provide a structure to bring many organizations and individuals to the crime prevention table. It's an accepted belief in policing that preventing family violence will lead to a reduction in street violence. Partnering police officers, prosecutors, civil attorneys, advocates, counselors, and medical professionals, brings critical public safety focus to family violence. This priority focus will bring the private and government funding needed to help victims and their children find the way forward after the abuse.
>
> John Welter, Chief of Police
> Anaheim Police Department/Anaheim Family Justice Center

creation. The principles include a commitment of a Center and its leaders to:

- Increase safety, promote healing, and foster empowerment through services for victims and their children

- Provide victim-centered services that promote victim autonomy

- Utilize culturally competent services approaches that are measurable and behavior based

- Engage all communities through outreach and community education

- Shape services to clients by asking them what they need

- Evaluate and adjust services by including survivor input

- Maintain close working relationships among all collaborators/agencies (law enforcement, prosecution, community-based domestic violence programs, shelters and other social services)

- Offer survivors a place to belong even after crisis intervention services are no longer necessary

- Integrate primary, secondary and tertiary prevention approaches into all initiatives, programs, and projects

- Develop a Family Justice Center Community that values, affirms, recognizes and supports staff, volunteers, and clients

Today, the Alliance has prioritized challenging Centers and all co-located service models that seek our assistance to embrace these principles and make them operational in the actions of the leadership and the activities of the partner agencies working in their collaborative models.

REMINDERS FOR A SUCCESSFUL COLLABORATIVE LEADER

David Archer and Alex Cameron have identified ten key lessons for successful collaborative leaders. All ten lessons have borne out in Family Justice Centers and they are worth highlighting here:

- Find the personal motive for collaborating

- Find ways of simplifying complex situations for your partners

- Prepare for how you are going to handle conflict well in advance

- Recognize that there are some people or organizations you can't work with!

- Have the courage to act for the long term

- Actively manage the tension between focusing on service delivery and building relationships (they are both critical)

- Invest in strong personal relationships at all levels

- Inject energy, passion, and drive into your leadership style

- Have the confidence to share the credit generously

- Continually develop your interpersonal skills, in particular: Empathy, patience, tenacity, holding difficult conversations, and coalition building.

Glen Aubrey recently focused on the nature of relationships in a Family Justice Center. "If I am personally committed to your success, and you are personally committed to my success, we have the basis for a strong working relationship. If my agency is committed to your agency's success, and your agency is committed to my agency's success, we will work well together."[5]

In many Family Justice Centers this has proved to be a maxim! If the lead agency in a Center wants all the credit and does not care about the success of its partner agencies, the Center will end up with very few partner agencies. If the Director is not regularly looking for ways to provide support to staff members from partner agencies, they will, sooner or later, leave the Center and discourage their agency from maintaining a presence at a Center.

To the list above, we must add a few other key qualities in successful FJC Directors—Humility, Sense of Humor, Ability to Forgive, and Domestic Violence Prevention Passion.

In my five years with the United States Marine Corps and 23 years with the FBI, I came to understand one of the fundamental elements of quality leadership is *candor*. A boss I once worked for was unhappy at a statement I'd made during a meeting with a variety of different law enforcement agencies gathered to address a sensitive issue. He felt someone in attendance could have been offended by my frankness. I responded, "Why must candor always be sacrificed on the altar of civility?" I do not believe that candor and civility are mutually exclusive; but the sacrificing of the former to achieve some sense of the latter often eliminates any opportunity to actually move an agenda forward. It was at that moment I decided a fundamental responsibility of a good leader is to ensure there exists, within their sphere of influence, an environment in which candor is not only *allowed*, but routinely *encouraged*. The best decisions are made when all relevant information is available to the decision maker. In an environment in which participants feel prohibited from speaking candidly, crucial information can be left out of the decision making process. It is never my intention to make anyone feel unnecessarily uncomfortable, but neither is it my intention to avoid a little discomfort at the cost of leaving critical information out of the discussion."

Michael M. Mason, Chief Security Officer, Verizon

Humility

There is nothing more damaging to a collaborative approach to reaching any goal or completing any project than arrogance and pride. So much of life comes down to whether I will when necessary surrender my own ego and my own pride for the good of a cause. Ronald Reagan often joked that we can get so much more done in life if we don't care who gets the credit. In the FJC world, this plays out regularly. If an FJC Director, or a District Attorney sponsoring a Center, or the head of the lead agency wants the credit and the glory, things usually don't go well. The Center may operate but partners are not personally invested and don't often engage fully because all the credit and all the glory must go to the lead agency, or the elected official, or the Director.

In contrast, when we have met strong leaders that maintain a servant's heart and make sure everybody gets recognized for their work we find Centers that thrive. Rebecca Lovelace, the Director of the Nampa Family Justice Center in Nampa, Idaho has proven in her years of leading one of the model Centers in the country that giving credit to others, sharing the awards and praise, and making sure she is constantly serving those she works with has demonstrated that your role as a leader is not compromised—it is enhanced. In New Orleans, no one doubts that Mary Claire Landry is in charge of Crescent House and the New Orleans Family Justice Center but her leadership approach always seeks to recognize the key partners, address their needs and concerns, and make sure that the Center is not about Mary Claire—it is about the victims and children that come to the Center for help.

Sense of Humor

We have rarely seen a Center Director last for a long time or thrive without a sense of humor. The ability to laugh at yourself and laugh when you want to cry is often a healthy coping mechanism in any part of our lives but in the tension-filled days of a Family Justice Center this is doubly true. It is a sensitive subject because the work of a Center is life and death every day. It is sobering to know that not properly assessing danger could lead to someone ending up in harm's way. The fear, terror, and trauma of the clients we serve is palpable during almost every interview, every legal consultation, and every counseling session. But your sense of humor may be one of your most powerful coping mechanisms. Research on resiliency, stress, and trauma has demonstrated the power of humor for many years.[6]

Abraham Lincoln during the darkest days of the Civil War, after a terrible report on the carnage burst out laughing and then looked at his advisors, none of whom were laughing, and said, "Gentleman, why don't you laugh? With the fearful strain that is upon me day and night, if I did not laugh I should die, and you need this medicine as much as I do." Wise words from a great leader! So as we evaluate leaders across the country in Family Justice Centers, we love to see laughter and humor. We love to see people who don't take themselves too seriously. And we love to see people who are able to laugh at themselves. It is the mark of a good leader.

Ability to Forgive

The third trait in successful FJC Directors beyond those traits we have identified in the research that apply in Family Justice Centers is the ability to forgive. Bitter, angry, resentful people rarely make good leaders. Those that hold grudges and find motivation to act from the wrongs that have been done to them are rarely good candidates for a job. Recently, Gael Strack and I interviewed someone for a job in San Diego that said "I am not really a team player and I have had a lot of people disrespect me so I enjoy working alone most of the time." Sadly, many people are that way but few people are willing to admit it. So, the challenge is to identify them before you hire them!

The willingness to forgive others and move on in life is a valuable talent. Often in collaboratives, as in life, people will mistreat an FJC Director, say inappropriate things because of stress, frustration, or anger. It is an intense work environment and the old adage of letting things roll off your back like "water off a duck's back" is a good one. If you are not able to do that, find another line of work. If you are look-ing for a Director, make sure you know how they deal with conflict and how they react when they are wronged. Probing before you hire them may save you a lot of pain after you hire them!

The Story of the Red Shoes

It was about 4:00 p.m. and I was just finishing a meeting in my office as the City Attorney of San Diego. The San Diego Family Justice Center had been open for over a year. The phone rang. It was Gael. Her voice was frantic. "We have a big problem," she said. My mind raced. Then she dropped the bomb: Someone with red shoes used the bathroom on the police floor at the Center without permission. I pondered her statement for a few seconds and then burst out laughing. Was this a joke? Gael was not laughing.

Within hours, the story became clear. The day before, a female detective in the Police Department's Domestic Violence Unit at the Center went to the restroom. Both stalls were being used. She noted the person in one of the stalls was wearing red shoes. Feeling put out, she used the stairwell to go to another floor and used that restroom. She returned to her desk and continued to fume. Had someone else used the Police Department bathroom without permission?

The detective got up from her desk and did a quick survey of the 6th floor. None of the detectives were wearing red shoes that day! It took astute detectives less than a day to get to the bottom of the red shoe mystery. The suspect was a victim advocate from the 7th floor; she had delivered a police report to a detective and had to use the bathroom before she returned to the community service floor where she worked. Within an hour of the conclusion of the manhunt—well, woman hunt—the inconvenienced detective had complained to her supervisor, and within two hours nearly 20 detectives were contemplating signing a grievance against the city, which would be forwarded to the Police Chief.

By the time Gael called me, the detectives wanted a formal apology from the city, and the whole idea of moving in together seemed like one very bad idea for providing hope to violent families everywhere. It took a few days to get to the bottom of the Hunt for Red (Shoes) October. But at the core of it all were small problems that had festered into big problems with some very angry police officers at the center of it all. Though laughable at first glance, this incident was much more complicated at its core than anyone could have imagined. And it was no laughing matter.

The grievance letter laid out the whole story. It had been nearly 18 months since the Center had opened. As already discussed, exposure on the Oprah Winfrey Show had brought site visitors from 49 states and 22 countries. Every day, strangers without identification and visitors without background checks streamed through the Center. No advance notice of tours was given. Everyone had access to every floor, and no one coordinated the site visits. They were conducted morning, noon, and night. On one visit, the lockers in the police officer area were fair game for tour members. Guests from another tour dined on food left in the kitchen area of the law enforcement floor. The grievance letter exposed a lack of security, violated privacy, and compromised work areas. In our excitement and exuberance to show off our innovative Center, we had violated the space of police officers and possibly others. It had little to do with the red shoes. It had everything to do with learning how to make a Center work.

Two weeks later, at a Center partners meeting, I stood before a large group of very angry detectives and apologized to them all. We had violated their work space, we had disrespected their values, and we needed to ensure that we would not do it again. One sincere apology from the guy in charge and the temperature in the room went down by 20 degrees. It was a lesson we would need to learn over and over again. When you make a mistake, apologize. When you need forgiveness, ask for it. When you have wronged somebody you live with, fess up to it! True in life, true in co-located service models...

The red shoes have become famous in the lore of the San Diego Family Justice Center. In fact, merely invoking the phrase *red shoes* is still a reminder to us all of the need to communicate, stay humble, keep our sense of humor, show grace and mercy, and address problems sooner rather than later. They were an unanticipated object lesson for anyone interested in taking coordinated community response strategies and collaboration to the level of moving in together in a specialized service facility. They will forever be the link between the concept and the reality of the Center.

Domestic Violence Prevention Passion

As we have watched Centers evolve and varying co-located models develop, we have also observed that it is very difficult for a Center to thrive if the first Director does not have a background in domestic violence services. The most successful Directors have worked in shelters, volunteered in community-based domestic violence organizations, or overcome violence and abuse in their own lives. Good leaders have emerged without this background but it is rare. Family Justice Centers at their core should be domestic violence focused collaboratives that also provide services to children exposed to violence and abuse. The co-located services model can work and even be effective without a close working relationship with community-based domestic violence agencies but it will rarely be vibrant and fully embody the heart and soul of the battered women's movement without a leader that has a strong working relationship with community-based domestic violence professionals.

If a new Director does not have a background in the domestic violence movement, they can obtain it and should reach out to the local shelter and the state domestic violence coalition quickly. They should obtain training in domestic violence dynamics, the history of the domestic violence movement, and should spend significant time with survivors of domestic violence.

This clear leadership issue is mitigated easily if the lead agency in a co-located services model is the local shelter or is a community-based domestic violence agency. But if the lead agency is not, this issue should be very carefully evaluated and addressed in the selection and training of a Center Director. Failure to understand this issue and address it has created real challenges for a number of Centers and has negatively impacted the Center's relationship with the local domestic violence shelter and the focus of the Center on developing a victim-centered approach to services and a service delivery model that is accountable to survivors of domestic violence.

POLITICAL LEADERSHIP MUST BE CULTIVATED

In many communities, planning for Centers and even the opening of a Center often starts with the support of a certain Mayor, Police Chief, District Attorney, or Shelter Director. Certain City Council members or County Commissioners are often the key leaders in helping to fund the start up and operation of a Center. Then, the Mayor leaves office. A new District Attorney or local prosecutor is elected. A new City Council comes along and the Family Justice Center was not their vision and is not their priority. Budgets get tight, finances are difficult. And the Family Justice Center ends up in the cross-hairs of budget cuts or staffing reductions. Political leadership matters too. The challenge of supporting the right people running for office and maintaining a close working relationship with them is not unique to the Family Justice Center or co-located services world.

In California, domestic violence shelters experienced this same painful journey under the leadership of Governor Arnold Schwarzenegger. They had always had the support of prior governors but Schwarzenegger eliminated, with his line item veto, all funding for domestic violence shelters. It was unthinkable and yet it happened. A leader who did not see funding for domestic violence programs as a priority and suddenly a life and death crisis of epic proportion.[7] The same thing has happened in Family Justice Center communities. Political leadership makes the Center happen and different leadership can put the Center in crisis.

The anti-dote, of course, to changing leadership is to cultivate on-going relationships with political candidates for office, to regularly brief local legislators on the successes of a Center, and share the credit with them for on-going effectiveness. Many Centers have created groups of survivors to regularly speak before local elected officials about the work of the Family Justice Center.[8] Other Centers produce regular reports that document their successes and keep all partners and all public officials apprised of the relevance of the Center's work to public safety. Many of these strategies are addressed in the practical workbooks produced by the National Family Justice Center Alliance.

But the overarching mission must be to maintain close relationships with a majority of the elected officials in a community that will be voting on the financial support necessary to operate a Family Justice Center or other type of coordinated or collaborative service delivery approach.

THE WRONG LEADER CAN SCREW IT ALL UP

A number of Centers, as noted earlier, have hired the wrong leader right from the beginning. There have been a host of reasons for picking someone who is not the right fit for the unique collaborative relationships that are necessary. Some communities have selected someone with no background in domestic violence when that community really needed someone who was personally invested in the movement. Others have hired a power and control/chain of command-type leader when they really needed someone who was able to work in a team environment. And others have hired passive aggressive or borderline personality disorder folks just because they wanted to get through the hiring process quickly or hire someone who would work long hours for low pay!

In one Center we have worked with, the first Director did excellent work. The next Director selected did not build on the work of the first Director. Not a bad person but the wrong fit for the job. The Center quickly lost partners, lost clients, and lost its commitment to best practices and accountability to survivors. And the actions of the wrong Director were relatively benign in isolation but incredibly destructive in the aggregate:

- Prohibited some partners from doing risk assessments

- Closed the Children's Room

- Ended a relationship with researchers

- Ended high risk case evaluations

- Eliminated Open Houses

- Stopped providing free parking for clients

- Terminated the planning for redecorating the Children's Room

- Stopped the Volunteer Academy

- Stopped assisting with efforts to fund the medical services

- Returned money to the federal government for medical services

- Ended Staff Appreciation Lunches and Awards Ceremonies

- Stopped all grant writing

- Stopped focus groups and exit interviews with clients

- Supported CPS Referrals

To magnify the problem, the wrong Director hired the wrong Operations Coordinator. Now, neither the Director nor the Operations Coordinator had any background in domestic violence and few relationships with people and agencies that had formed the foundation of the community's work in family violence.

The wrong Operations Coordinator began to report FJC clients to Child Welfare Services whenever their children had witnessed violence. It was disastrous. It did not take long for the word to get out that the FJC was not a safe place for women to come for help. The client load dropped dramatically to less than 100 clients per month in less than a year. On-site partner agencies went from 21 down to 10 in a matter of six months.

Finally, the partners had to raise objection, call for a change in leadership, and rally together to get a different Director. The Police Department served as the lead agency in that Center and then appointed a strong, collaborative leader and committed to rebuilding the Center and restoring best practices in every aspect of the operation. But the lesson should not be lost, the partners had to stick together, organize, stand up to the wrong leader, and go above the Director to maintain the vision and work of the Center.

Today, that Center is thriving again with a dedicated Director and Operations Coordinator who both have a strong history in working with domestic violence and sexual assault victims. Local domestic violence shelters are fully engaged and the Family Justice Center Alliance has been brought in to help promote best practices, a clear focus on accountability to survivors, and a commitment to honoring the guiding principles of the Family Justice Center movement.

Multiple Centers have experienced the wrong leader and experienced the same journey described in just one particular Center. The damage happens fast. The re-building process takes much longer. But the lessons learned are clear: Pick the right leader; Maintain strong political support; Cultivate healthy relationships among all the partners; Hold each other accountable when things go wrong; and then keep re-committing to innovative approaches and constant re-invention as the partnership evolves over time.

CONCLUSION

Leadership matters. One person can screw it all up. Building and maintaining strong, close personal relationships will preserve a Center. In the next chapter, we will talk about the other big lessons from Centers that have struggled—other than the leadership issue—and look at how these lessons can point the way forward for Centers in the future. There are challenges in any organization, in any co-located services model, in any coordinated community response. The difference between failure and success is the ability to identify the challenges and properly address them. It is the focus of Chapter 8.

NOTES

1 See Glen Aubrey, *Lincoln, Leadership, and Gettysburg: Defining Moments of Greatness*, (2009), Creative Team Publishing.

2 Phillip H. Eastman, *The Character of Leadership: An Ancient Model for the Quantum Age*, (2009)

3 See http://www.youtube.com/watch?v=CQ0vdJrl45A

4 Presentation by Madeleine Carter, National Exploited and Missing Persons Conference, July 27, 2005, Philadelphia, Pennsylvania.

5 Interview with Glen Aubrey, January 2010—National Family Justice Center Alliance Offices, San Diego, CA.

6 See Martin, R.A. and Lefcourt, H.M (1983) "Sense of Humor as a Moderator of the Relation Between Stressors and Moods," *Journal of Personality and Social Psychology*, 45, pp. 1313-1324.

7 The Governor twice eliminated funding for shelters in California—first by line item veto in 2009, and then by removing funding for shelters in his proposed budget in 2010.

8 The San Diego FJC first created its VOICES Committee in 2006. The committee is made up of former FJC clients and survivors that advocate for the Center and host special events for survivors and their children. Many other Centers are now creating VOICES Committees as well including New Orleans (LA), Nampa (ID), Defiance (OH), Knoxville (TN), and others. For more information, go to: www.nfjcavoices.org.

CHAPTER EIGHT

Challenges in Family Justice Centers

Gael and her team were in the middle of one of our first focus group of 20 clients who had received services at the Center. The conversation covered the expected range of personal experiences, including which services were utilized and which were not. At the end of our focus group, the most remarkable question came from a client named Della. "What took you so long?" It stopped everyone in their tracks. Gael glanced at the other professionals with her—Judi Adams, a Strategic Planner, and Kimberly Pearce, the Director of Client Services. They all understood the implications of Della's question. It reached far beyond the walls of San Diego's Family Justice Center. Della simply wanted to know what took so long to open the Center. She continued, "If only this place had been here just five years ago, my life would be so different. And my children's lives would have been different."

Della said that five years earlier she did not know where to turn. She had no place to go. She didn't want to testify in court. In fact, she actively avoided testifying in court. She ignored calls from criminal justice agencies and dodged subpoenas. She wanted help from social service agencies but had lost the sheet of paper the police officer gave her. She tried to call 411 to find those agencies, but they kept referring her to the wrong place.

Nobody answered at some numbers and others were disconnected. She became frustrated and gave up. Her husband was threatening her on a daily basis. He said if she dared to show up in court to testify against him, he would get even with her. He promised to make her life miserable and do everything he could to take her children away. Della felt she had no options. She had to go back for the sake of her children. She was tired of trying to figure it all out.

When she returned, she knew nothing had changed despite her husband's promises and tears. Della told the focus group, "He continued to make my life miserable. I'm tired of him getting away with it. That's why I'm back here with another case. But this time, it's different. You're all here at one place. It's much easier now. And I just want to know what took you so long to figure this out? Don't you know we've all been waiting for a long time for something like the Family Justice Center?"

Gael wrote in our first book: "Della's question still sends chills up my spine and it energizes our efforts to continue expanding the Center. It's that one question that repeatedly came up in the early focus groups: What took San Diego so long to co-locate all the professionals under one roof to make it easier for victims and families struggling with domestic violence? From that moment forward, we were humbled by the realization that there were thousands of hurting families that needed us to figure it out and get it right."

This chapter is partly an answer to Della. The reason comprehensive co-located services models took so long is because they are very complicated and getting everyone to work together and then live together is really, really complicated. There are many difficulties and challenges that must be addressed and overcome to make it all work.

So, let's get down to the difficulties of the Family Justice Center concept, let's talk about the challenges in some Family Justice Centers, why one has closed since the movement began, and what you need to know that we usually don't like to talk about as we celebrate, and praise, and hail the good parts of the movement toward co-located, multi-agency services. Since the movement has begun, we have kept track of what goes wrong, we have provided technical assistance to struggling Centers, and we have helped communities work through some painful issues in their Centers. In Chapter 7, we talked about the critical importance of leadership. To be sure, many of the issues we will talk about here also connect at some level to leadership, but let's put it all out there with the book theme in mind—Family Justice Centers are complicated.

Here is a list of the big issues in unhealthy or struggling Family Justice Centers:

- Power and control

- Personality conflicts

- Turf battles

- Withdrawal

- Refusal to work together

- Isolation

- Ego conflicts

- Inappropriate responses to stress

- Poor anger management

- Poor communication

- Financial issues

- Undealt with grievances or mistreatment

- Disrespect

- Selfishness

- Gossip

- Jealousy

Does the list look familiar? It looks a little bit like unhealthy, abusive relationships! And the list is not totally unfamiliar to anyone working in any agency, organization, or business. The list is not unfamiliar to anyone who has had struggles on the board of a non-profit organization or has been caught in the conflicts in a church, mosque, or synagogue. Shelters can struggle with these issues. Other community-based nonprofit agencies can struggle with these issues. A lot of families end up struggling with many of these even if there is no physical abuse in a family. This is probably a list of things that could be applied to almost any group of human beings almost anywhere at some time. It should not be shocking that Family Justice Centers have the same issues when you bring together human beings with their own issues, pain, struggles, and baggage.

And you see the irony, right? Our unhealthy, dysfunctional agencies all get together and then tell unhealthy, dysfunctional families to come to us for help! A very pathetic picture indeed! I often joke that if there were no human beings and no agencies involved, Family Justice Centers would be pretty simple. But imperfect human beings tend to mess everything up!

If multi-agency co-location can magnify the positive benefits of a coordinated community response, it can also magnify the negatives. Agencies may have issues with each other but if they don't have to see each other every day, they can usually ignore them. People may offend one another or rub each other the wrong way at times, but if they are working together day in and day out—in a high stress, difficult environment—the issues will probably be more obvious. If gossip can spread like wildfire in a company, an organization, a church, or a social group, imagine how fast it can spread among 20 agencies all working in the same place!

DIFFERENT CULTURES AND DIFFERENT ORGANIZATIONAL VALUES CREATE CHALLENGES AND OBSTACLES

Beyond, the basic interpersonal issues that crop up in Family Justice Centers because of our humanity, there are also other cultural issues. If you have 25 strong, independent, dynamic, driven, focused agencies with staff members in one place, you have a great force for positive social change. But you also have 25 strong, independent, driven, focused agencies that don't easily want to associate with each other, listen to other, or work to find common ground with others. Organizational culture varies greatly from police departments, to prosecutor's offices, to hospitals, to churches, to feminist domestic violence organizations, to child welfare departments, to the courts, to social service agencies, and to other types of organizations.

Many law enforcement agencies have a chain of command structure and then they come and join a collaborative that is not a top-down organization. Many social service organizations try hard to be less chain of command and more egalitarian. But egalitarian is inefficient when a crisis happens and decisions need to be made quickly. Talking about these differences and regularly sharing can help address these kinds of conflicts but when case volume is high and the day to day work is always pressing, people don't often want to take the time to talk. One police officer in a Center said soon after it opened, "I hope I don't have to share my feelings every day. It will drive me crazy."[1] You might have guessed it…a male cop moving into a shelter-led FJC had a little bit of an attitude! But it could just as easily be a female cop or a doctor or a prosecutor that arrives in an FJC with a different world view than a counselor or social worker.

MAKE SURE EVERYBODY IS MOVING IN THE SAME DIRECTION

Some Centers have had major struggles because of their structure. In St. Louis (MO), the FJC organized around a non-profit entity that had the heads of all the local non-profits at the Board. Each non-profit had to raise their own money, fund their own organizations, and promote their own identity in the community. They had little interest in promoting the St. Louis Family Justice Center. With competing agencies and competing priorities, once the federal grant ran out that started the Center, there was no sustainability plan, no organized group of champions for the Center, and little to do but close it down.

Other Centers have found that if their lead agency is a shelter,

the government funding and support tends to wane over time and
there is a natural tendency for the government to be less interested in
on-going funding because it is viewed less as a public safety initiative
and more as another social service program. As discussed in Chapter
7, this is often connected to changing leaders in local or state government. One generation of leaders may have supported the vision and
felt invested but the next generation, if not fully engaged and culti-
vated, will not view the project as their own and will not feel invested
in its success.

Community-based domestic violence and sexual assault agencies are the
heart and soul of a social change movement that has now recruited many
more partners, disciplines, and service providers to end violence in our
communities. Community-based domestic violence and sexual assault
agencies must continue to engage new and long standing allies as we
propose new ideas, and try to improve on meeting the needs of victims and
their children. Private and public partnerships that include law enforcement
entities and prosecutors must be continued to sustain, enhance and/or
build a coordinated community response. These public and private partnerships rely on each other to work effectively to serve victims who reach
out for help. Strong partnerships help challenge all of the entities to remove
barriers to services and to be more creative and client-centered. When the
time is right, co-location is a powerful way to multiply the effectiveness of
collaboration.

Verna Griffin Tabor
Executive Director
Center for Community Solutions

The other iteration of this issue has played out in Centers when
there is a shelter-based lead agency that is "sponsoring" or managing
the Family Justice Center but they don't see it as integral to their own
operation. When this happens, the FJC tends to become an annoy-
ance or a competitor to the lead agency and is not allowed to seek the
needed funds, to develop an independent identity, or to really spread
its wings and get out into the community. A number of Centers led
by shelters are thriving such as Ouachita Parish (LA), Indianapolis
(IN), Salt Lake City (UT), and others. But there is clearly a pattern
that occurs when the lead agency does not fully embrace the vision for

the Family Justice Center and don't let it become the powerful entity it can become in a community.

DON'T DO 'PAY TO PLAY'

A few Centers, usually those associated with elected or public policy makers, have adopted a "pay to play" approach and have attempted to charge rent to partner agencies if they want to participate. One Center in Boise (ID) went down this road and quickly found they had alienated most of the local service providers and non-profits who struggle to pay the bills every month. If the choice is making payroll or moving into a Family Justice Center, most agencies will choose to pay their employees and tell the FJC to pound sand. This same dynamic could happen if the lead agency is a non-profit as well and simply wants other agencies to "pay their fair share" of the costs of co-location.

The best approach to this is always to see the FJC as a public safety initiative and ensure that a significant portion of the building (leasing costs and operating expenses) or buildings to be used is borne by the city or county government. The least expensive way to go is to use an existing government building so that only operating expenses have to be raised instead of rent cost. In Boston, the Mayor provided the building free of charge which dramatically reduced operating costs. In Alameda County, District Attorney Nancy O'Malley successfully lobbied for the use of a county-owned building. In many Centers, the local government has picked up the leasing costs if they must rent space. Montgomery (AL) recently used public funds from the City and County to buy a building for the Center to ensure its existence for the long-term and reduce month to month expenses that would have accrued in a rented building.

But the Centers that have gotten into trouble around 'pay to play' or the covering of basic costs have usually ended up in a situation where the organizers or sponsors forget that this is a public safety initiative and should have major core funding coming from local government. Federal grants can help but they come and go. Major fundraising and philanthropic support is helpful as well. But the core operating expenses need to be borne by the government entities that will pay $500,000 - $2,500,000 to handle the murders when intervention fails. They are the ones that will have to lock up the next generation of children growing up in domestic violence homes without effective intervention. They are the primary entities that must help to move the money from the back end of the system to the front end of the system.

DON'T IGNORE THE LOCAL SHELTER, COORDINATING COUNCIL, OR STATE COALITION

In communities where the local shelter is the lead agency for a Family Justice Center, the relationship with the state domestic violence coalition usually remains fairly strong and reaps dividends for the FJC and the shelter. Even if they might have some philosophical differences on certain issues, their close working relationship helps maintain healthy interaction. In our first every statewide Family Justice Initiative funded by Blueshield of California Foundation, we required all new Centers whether shelter-led or not to be members of the Alliance and maintain open lines of the communication with the state coalition. Sue Else, the President of the National Network to End Domestic Violence has said it well: "Staying close to your state coalition is a positive thing. Including coalitions in your local FJC or coordinating council will make your agency more effective and lend you valuable resources and support."

Sadly, some local shelters have not engaged in FJC development processes in some communities and this is a loss for victims and all the partner agencies. Family Justice Center communities should always seek to include local shelter programs in any planning process whether the shelter will have a primary role or a lead role in a Center or not. If a local shelter director chooses not to participate, there is little the other agencies can do to compel her but the offer to participate should always be extended and NEVER withdrawn. Not all victims of domestic violence utilize the services of a local shelter or transitional housing program but emergency, safe housing is central to keeping some victims safe and long-term housing is almost always a critical issue for survivors. Survivors lose when shelters refuse to partner with a local FJC and survivors lose when an FJC refuses to work closely with their local shelter.

> The relationship between Valley Crisis Center and the Nampa FJC is nothing short of a miracle. The services that we have been able to provide the community, I believe, have been able to save women's lives. Even when there have been bumps in the road, we have been able to work them out to the benefit of everyone, especially survivors. The important thing to remember when working as a partner with the FJC is communication. Remember that we are here to help survivors, not stroke our own egos. There is always room for improvement and we will continue to strive for excellence when it comes to saving lives.
>
> **Yolanda Matos, Executive Director**
> **Valley Crisis Center**

In San Diego, the local coordinating council, that included all the local shelters, played a powerful role in creating the San Diego Family Justice Center. Conversely, a failure to include the Council and the shelters would have made creating a healthy co-located services model very difficult.

Centers that have ignored their roots or failed to understand the central importance of the domestic violence movement in their very existence rarely do well in the long-run. And they miss out on the many valuable lessons that the domestic violence movement has learned in trying to provide co-located or multi-disciplinary services, in trying to change systems and structures, and in generally working to meet the needs of victims and their children. In Chapter 2, on the history of the domestic violence movement, we heard the story of Mr. Know It All. Don't forget his very bad example! He probably didn't have a relationship with his state domestic violence coalition and I doubt he even knew whether there was a local domestic violence co-ordinating council.

BAD THINGS HAPPEN WHEN SERVICES ARE NOT VICTIM-CENTERED

A whole host of issues and challenges have been identified in Family Justice Centers around issues of victim-centered services. When a Family Justice Center or any service organization stops listening to victims and stops letting victims make their own choices bad things tend to happen over time.

Don't Become a Benevolent Batterer

I often call it the benevolent batterer syndrome when our systems start ordering victims around. They come to us for help to escape an abuser who is ordering them around and dictating what they can and cannot do. And then we start ordering them around in our agencies. We don't physically abuse them. We are more benevolent. We may threaten to take their kids, hold them in contempt in court, or blame them for the abuse they have suffered because they have not left yet. But we don't physically hit them. It is the benevolent batterer syndrome...and it is an ugly way to help hurting families.

Some Centers tend to become very authoritarian and clinical in their approach to service delivery. When this happens, victims get told what to do instead of getting to choose what they do. They get told which partners they are going to see instead of being in charge of their own journey toward healing. Whenever paternalism starts to creep in to any agency serving victims and their children, bad things start to happen. Court systems often tend toward paternalism, prosecutor's offices and police departments lean this way, and child welfare services have a natural bent toward this approach. But it can happen in a shelter, a community-based domestic violence agency, or a social service center-based model as well.

Using power and control with a victim of power and control will not solve the problem of power and control they are experiencing! But we see it in Centers from time to time. This does not mean that you ignore the law. If you have medical mandated reporting of domestic violence, you need to let victims know that up front if they are going to be asking for medical services and have not called the police. If you have mandatory reporting obligations for child abuse, you need to let them know that up front. If certain agencies have mandatory reporting obligations and others at a Center don't, victims have a right to know that as well. Then, if they want to get services at an agency that will not report them, they need to be transported to that agency. No, not simply referred! A full-service Center will transport them there or have that agency come over the pick them up.

Listen to Survivors and Don't Stop Listening...Ever!
Many Centers have struggled with keeping up focus groups and exit interviews with every client they serve. They start out very victim-centered and then it fades away in the crush of every day crises and challenges. Sooner or later, when you stop listening, your Center will not be victim-centered in its approach. This can happen at a shelter, a community-based domestic violence agency, or a Family Justice Center. Victims who experience our agencies and our systems should be empowered to tell us how we are doing. We give them real respect when we are responsive to their expressed concerns. I serve on the board of a domestic violence shelter that has "empowerment" as one of our goals but early on in my tenure it seemed to me that we acted as if empowerment is something we do to someone instead of something we help them do for themselves. We had too many rules, too many consequences for breaking stupid rules, and too many contract provisions they had to agree to or we would kick them out of our program. That approach is not empowerment! Not coincidentally, the organization could not remember that last time it had done regular focus groups with clients to get their feedback and re-evaluate our service delivery model.

Clients in Family Justice Centers quickly know if they are respected and empowered to be part of the successful work of a Center or not. If they are invited to focus groups every quarter, if they offered exit interviews every time they visit, if they are invited to join a VOICES Committee (former FJC clients) at the Center—they know they are respected and the Center is victim-centered. If they come in and get told what to do, get treated as "less than" in any way, or are ignored or marginalized—they figure out very quickly that the Center is looking down on them and doing things to them instead of doing things for them. Centers that stop listening eventually lose their way and suffer the consequences for it in the long-run.

CHANGE AND GROW OR STAGNATE AND SHRIVEL

As Centers in the FJC movement start reaching the 5-7 year mark, they are experiencing some of the same issues as many organizations and are living testimonies to the organizational development principles that many have identified.[2] Service organizations or collaborative teams or corporations all have a development journey. In the beginning, things are exciting. There is energy and creativity. Passion substitutes for procedures and a sense of newness masks the need for structure. But over time, the zeal wears off or the zealots leave, and the revolution is over. Now, the managers arrive. The new community must be governed. And things change. It is hard to keep up the energy level, the excitement level, and the adrenalin level. It is in this difficult time that many Centers tend toward a focus on compliance with policies and procedures. Other Centers seem to be willing to compromise on best practices or the time consuming effort that went in to constant re-evaluation of every process in the first five years.

The adage our Board Chair, Mike Scogin, offers in the face of these challenges is "Change and grow, or stagnate and shrivel." Many Centers are disappointed to find out that once they open it is not the finish line they have reached, it is the starting line! Now the real work begins, now the challenge of making the ideas come alive day in and day out is fully engaged. And as time goes by, you have to keep evolving, changing, and growing. There is no such thing as a healthy status quo in a Family Justice Center or in virtually any organization. The mission statement for the organization has to embrace change as a critical value and then the value has to be implemented. This runs counter to the thinking of a struggling non-profit just trying to get by or protect their little piece of the pie (in funding terms). It runs counter to the thinking of a bureaucratic organization that rarely emphasizes the importance of constant change and evolution as one of its most treasured values. But "change and grow, or stagnate and shrivel" must be the clarion call of Family Justice Centers.

The National Family Justice Center Alliance has now created a Snapshot Process[3] to evaluate a community that is planning a Center or to assess an operating Center. The Snapshot Process, including focus groups with survivors, on-line surveys with partner agencies, and the associated 34 page tool that is used with a Center's leadership or planning committee helps us evaluate the health of a community's coordinated response and their actual operations if the Center is underway. When we find problems with Centers that earlier did not have similar problems, it is usually because policies or procedures that were put in place at the beginning are no longer being followed. We often identify good things they did at the beginning but they did not keep evolving them, evaluating them, and changing them as time passed. We hear people say, "We used to do that", or "When that agency was here they did that." It quickly becomes apparent that they stopped innovating, they stopped trying new things, they stopped evolving. Faced with the reality of changing and evolving or shriveling, they have slowly started to shrivel.

My father-in-law often says "When you have more memories than dreams, you have begun to die." The statement is also true in Family Justice Centers. Centers that are thriving are constantly looking for new ideas, new partners, and new approaches. Healthy Centers are looking for ways to improve things or modify existing operations to make them better for victims and their children. Centers that are sliding backwards have stopped dreaming, stopped aspiring, and stopped looking for ways to do even better. There is no exception.

EMBRACE THE ANTI-DOTE OR PULL THE PLUG

A chapter on how things go bad would not be complete without talking about how you stop the disease, how you counteract the poison that can destroy a Family Justice Center, a domestic violence shelter, or any other kind of organization. As we provide training and technical assistance in Centers, we often put up a list of what helps Centers address their problems and deal with their illnesses. It might be a familiar list for anyone who has ever studied what healthy relationships look like:

- Giving grace to others

- Giving and receiving mercy

- Being honest

- Forgiving

- Staying committed to excellence

- Practicing humility

- Acting unselfishly

- Maintaining a sense of humor

- Soaking each other in affirmation

- Offering encouragement

- Always giving respect

- Living in the moment

- Remembering to dream

- Sharing resources

- Massive amounts of communication

We know that when unhealthy relationship dynamics play out in organizations of any kind, bad things happen, as we saw at the beginning of the chapter. When healthy relationship dynamics play out, good things happen.

But as we often remind leadership teams and partner agencies in Centers—life is all about choices. Agencies and individuals have to be willing to choose these values and these patterns of behavior. A Director who has onsite partners that are acting in unhealthy ways either needs to help them change their approach or ask them to leave. If an agency is not helping a dynamic in a Center, perhaps they need to leave. In our "how to" manuals we address this issue regarding how to structure partnership agreements and the ability of the Director or Operations Committee to have a partner leave. In any collaborative team that lasts for a long time, partners will come and go. This has been true in Family Justice Centers. Sometimes they come because they get a new grant. Sometimes they leave because they lose a grant. Sometimes they come because there is a close relationship between that agency and certain partner agencies. Other times they leave because an agency is not playing well in the sandbox. But is it very clear that when a Director is monitoring partner relationships and has his/her hand on the pulse of the Center every day, you can address issues when they are small and not wait until they become monsters. Centers that have gotten in trouble have gone too far down the road of not addressing problems or problem relationships and the pain and trauma when they do finally deal with them can cause major repercussions in the effectiveness of a Center.

CONCLUSION

When things go bad in a Family Justice Center, it is usually about relationships, leadership, or structure. Centers are not really that different from most other organizations in that human beings bring their own issues and baggage to work every day. The problems are compounded, however, with different organizational cultures attempting to come together. Staying focused on the vision is usually the best anti-dote along with a healthy dose of forgiveness, grace, respect, and humility. Della reminded us a long time ago that she and many other survivors of domestic violence need us to figure out the challenges in our communities and in Gael Strack's words, "Get it right."

NOTES

1   Gael Strack has presented many times on the culture and value differences in multi-disciplinary work. She brought together and kept together 120 professionals from 27 different agencies for more than five years at the San Diego FJC from 2002-2007. For a webcast training on this very topic, go to www.familyjusticecenter.org/ResourceLibrary.

2   See Gwinn, Strack, Adams, Lovelace, Norman, *"The Family Justice Center Collaborative Model,"* St. Louis University Public Law Review Vol. XXVII 79 (2007), for a deeper discussion of these issues.

3   The FJC Snapshot Process was originally funded by the Blue Shield of California Foundation as part of its California Family Justice Initiative. The Snapshot Process is implemented at a Center or in a community planning a Center by the NFJCA Team when working with a local community to provide technical assistance, strategic planning support, or community evaluation of readiness for a Center. For more information, go to: www.familyjusticeinitiative.org.

CHAPTER NINE

Why the Whole World Needs a Family Justice Center

My name is Sana. I was born in Jordan, in the City of Ajloun. I married and had a son but by the age of 27, I was divorced after suffering constant abuse. I was forced to return home to my family. I only completed sixth grade so obtaining a job was difficult and I remained unemployed and financially dependent on my family. I received only JD20 monthly alimony from my husband after battling in court to obtain child support. On many occasions, he does not pay me on time. My family has practiced all forms of pressure on me to return my child to my husband. My family forced me to marry another man so that someone would be responsible for me and my child.

At my new marriage home, I faced even worse living conditions than with my first husband. Again, I was physically and mentally abused as well as deprived from leaving the house. My husband attempted to isolate me from others and forbade me from talking on the phone with my friends and neighbors. My child was also abused by his step-father.

The step-father would say things to my son like "Sit down, you dog... you are an idiot like your father...if your mother did not do something wrong she would not have been divorced."

My abusive husband would say things like: "If you were a good woman your husband would have not divorced you and your family would have not gotten rid of you by marrying you off to me." My husband often made it clear to me that he married me so that I would serve him and his children. With few resources and services, I am forced to depend on my abusive husband and bear his constant abuse. Where would I go for help?

The story that begins this chapter is from Amman, Jordan. In the early stages of planning the first two Family Justice Centers in the Middle East in Amman, Jordan, we encouraged our local team to conduct focus groups and listen to survivors. Sana's story emerged early in the process. It was a familiar story. Sana's experience was similar to stories we have heard all over the world. It was more difficult to address her plight because there are fewer services in Jordan, the cultural forces that keep victims in the home are much more powerful, and the social options if they try to leave are much more limited. But the experience of trying to get help in the face of power and control and a myriad of obstacles was familiar. The story was familiar to the ones we had heard in the United States, Mexico, Canada, Great Britain, Western Europe, Eastern Europe, Asia, Australia, New Zealand, and many other places around the world. And the worst is yet to come as more awareness leads to more resources and more resources leads to more places where a victim has to go for help in more places around the world. It is the reason this chapter is in the book. We need co-located, multi-agency service delivery models around the world.

FAMILY JUSTICE CENTER MODELS IN OTHER COUNTRIES

Now nearly a decade into the Family Justice Center movement, we have many different models of co-location emerging around the world. And each of them proves the point of this chapter.

Waterloo-Kitchener

Cathy Brothers, Pam Mank, and Sean Tout in the province of Ontario have done an amazing job of developing a Family Justice Centre model for Canada. Under the leadership of Catholic Fam-

ily Services, they have co-located shelter services, housing, legal services, police services, and a host of social services under one roof. It
is a beautiful complex. The entire collaborative is now called Mosaic
Counseling and Family Services. They figured out how to get along,
they figured out how to blend cultures, and they figured out how to
get all the agencies to stick together.

Hope and safety for victims of family violence in Waterloo Region, Ontario,
Canada have become much closer to reality as a result of Casey Gwinn's
and Gael Strack's vision of many systems and sectors working together. In
2005 we heard Casey's passionate commitment to changing the lives of
women and children who live with the terror of domestic violence. We were
inspired by Casey's brilliant, common sense model of co-located services.
In January 2006, the newly formed Domestic Violence Unit of Waterloo
Region Police Services and the Crown Attorney assigned to domestic violence moved into the beautiful facilities of Mosaic Counselling and Family Services, a non-government, voluntary organization. They joined the
hospital-based Sexual Assault and Domestic Violence Treatment Centre,
who were already tenants of Mosaic. Within a short period of time fifteen
organizations with a mandate to address issues of family violence had co-
located at Mosaic and a successful two million dollar capital campaign
was launched, with former President Bill Clinton as Guest Speaker, to expand Mosaic's building. The Family Violence Project of Waterloo Region
was embraced by the community from the outset. The respectful, diverse,
and positive culture of Mosaic continues to support the uniqueness of each
of the co-located partners. This project is truly an example of Casey and
Gael's co-located model working where none of the partners give up their
governance or administration; but, all work together to reach the shared
goals of truly supporting victims of domestic violence.

Cathy Brothers, Former Executive Director
Mosaic Counseling and Family Services (Waterloo, Ontario)

Gael and I visited their Center a number of times and I was im-
pressed. One day I was there it was a community outreach day for the
Afghan community. The men were in one meeting room, the women
were in another. They were not there for family violence services.
They were there to socialize because the Center had made their facility available for free. As we briefly toured each room, and I greeted
the men in one room and the women in another, I asked one of the

interpreters what each group was talking about. He said the men are talking about what they think the women are talking about! And then he said the women are talking about violence and abuse. Wow. This amazing Center, based in a domestic violence shelter, was changing the world for the Afghan community in Waterloo-Kitchener. They were using their facility for community outreach. They are educating victims about the existence of their programs by simply welcoming them into their facilities, serving them food, and showing them hospitality. But they were doing what we want Family Justice Centers in the U.S. to start doing. They were combining prevention with intervention with powerful results.

> It is not reasonable to expect women, and/or service providers for that matter, to access and make sense of a multitude of potentially unknown services in unknown locations at a time of high stress, anxiety and danger. Co-ordination, communication, and co-location are not the entire solution to end domestic violence but these elements are fundamental and critical components. Our clients do not ask us about our philosophical view points, our mandates, or our funding base. They only ask us if we can help them. We must get past our differences and recognize that it is about serving and answering, "yes", to the question of our ability to help. Success should not be measured by whether a client stays or leaves the relationship, rather measured by the amount of support that clients receive and that they feel safe and know where to reach out in future. Together we do and will continue to make a difference.
>
> Pamela Mank, MSW, RSW
> Assistant Clinical Director/Coordinator
> Family Violence Project of Waterloo Region

South Africa

Synnov Skorge is the Director of the Saartjie Baartman Centre for Women and Children in Manenberg, South Africa. She is a powerful advocate for the Family Justice Center movement in Africa. I met her at the United Nations a number of years ago and she shared with me her passion for our work and vision…from half way around the world. The Saartjie Baartman Centre for Women and Children (SBCWC) was opened in 1999 as the first multi-disciplinary service (one-stop) centre for abused women and children in the country. This provided an opportunity for organizations to come together as partners to develop an appropriate on-site multi-agency service delivery model for the effective management, treatment and prevention of violence against women and children. It also presented an opportunity for a partnership approach between government departments and the non-governmental sector. It is the first Center in Africa that fully fits the concept of a Family Justice Center.[1]

The Saartjie Baartman Centre is a much needed resource for women and children in South Africa. The level of gender-based violence is horrifically high and more centres such as the Saartjie Baartman centre are urgently needed. Women and children experiencing violence in their lives need a multi—layered response. The centre is also effective in its advocacy and lobbying work.

Synnov Skorge, Director
Saartjie Baartman Centre for Women and Children
Manenberg, South Africa

The Centre has since evolved to be the prime learning site in South Africa for providing holistic, integrated services to survivors of violence. Some of the services provided are managed directly by the Saartjie Baartman Centre. These include a 24-hour crisis response; a residential shelter and transitional housing for abused women and their children; legal assistance; and job-skills training. The other services are provided by partner organizations with staff assigned to and working at the Centre and include an after-hours crisis response for children; specialized counseling services in rape/sexual assault, drug and alcohol abuse, trauma and domestic violence; job-skills training and job placement projects; HIV/AIDS programs; community outreach; advocacy and lobbying; training; and research. Law enforcement officials come to the Center on an on-call basis though they are not co-located.

The Center clearly has a shelter-based, gender-based approach to co-located, multi-agency services. Though this has made it difficult to fully engage the law enforcement sector in South Africa, it is another excellent example of how the model looks differently in different places around the world.

Great Britain

The Family Justice Centre vision in the United Kingdom began with a Police Commander named Steve Allen. He was joined by a social services policy advocate named Jill Maddison and by Police Commander Mark Gore. These visionaries in Croydon, borough south of London, helped launch the budding Family Justice Center movement in the U.K. Croydon became the first Centre, operating out of rented office space near the courthouse. But the key component in Croydon was the commitment of Scotland Yard and the Metropolitan Police to collaborating with non-governmental organizations. Without such a police commitment, the movement never could have gotten underway. On one of our first visits to the Center, we were struck by the powerful commitment from local elected officials from the Croydon Council. They "got it" at a very early stage in the process and their leadership and willingness to spend money launched the movement.

> The Family Justice Centre concept is a powerful way to help victims and their children. When we come together in such a model, we are more powerful, victims are more powerful, and abusers lose power. Everyone working together increases accountability for the offender and increases the chances that the violence will not continue. The great challenge is for each community to determine how they can come together and stay together, completely focused on the vision of helping those who need us.
>
> Steve Allen
> Former Commander, Metropolitan Police Service, New Scotland Yard
> Deputy Chief Constable Lothian and Borders Police

Croydon also helped us see how we can learn from others in this journey toward more effective co-located services. We created a sister-city relationship between Croydon and San Diego. We engaged in numerous trips back and forth. We visited them multiple times. They visited us on numerous occasions—they learned and we learned.

> I was very skeptical of coming here when I first started because I was a policeman. It took me about six months here to get used to the idea of working with everyone else. But now I would champion the cause to anybody in the world because I think the Family Justice Centre is better than sliced bread. It will eventually, not solve the problem, but make a major dent in the problem for victims and their children.
>
> Detective Alex Starr
> Metropolitan Police Service - Croydon

Croydon also taught me another lesson. Jill Maddison, Mark Gore, and the team in Croydon created a client appreciation luncheon to honor victims of domestic violence. What a powerful way to show respect and honor in the process of hosting co-located services for victims and their children. I had the opportunity to be there for one such luncheon with Gael. There must have been 40 survivors mingling with police officers, prosecutors, advocates, counselors, and others. The children were playing in the children's room at the Center (and running everywhere!). It was magic. I talked to a number of survivors during the event. They felt like celebrities. They felt like the guests of honor at a special banquet. What a great reminder of how simple ideas can have such powerful results. Gael took photos of the event, careful not to take any photos of the faces of the clients. But before she knew it, women were approaching her, asking her to take photos of them and their children. She easily spent the next hour taking photos of clients and their children until they just couldn't smile anymore. We had never seen anything like it! We had to know why they wanted photos and they told us. They said they had fled their homes with their photos left behind as they fled for their lives. Many said their abusers had destroyed photos of themselves and their children. One woman, stood before Gael, holding a box in her hands, and explained that she had all her photos in that box. The photos were her treasure. At that moment, we were inspired to go back home and not only invite our clients to appreciation luncheons but also launch our Portraits of Courage Project and take photos of our clients and their children whenever they asked us!

Monterrey, Mexico

Aiaxa Alvarado is a determined woman who founded the first Family Justice Center in Mexico—Centro de Justicia Familiar. She has overcome the odds. She has persevered through many challenges and difficult circumstances. But with few resources, turf issues, competition among agencies, and a challenging court system and criminal justice response, she has become one of my heroes. The first Center in Mexico was supported by President Vicente Fox and set a standard for Children's Rooms. It was one of the first Centers to ask victims during the design process about their access to their children while receiving services. They said they wanted to see them but not necessarily be with them. So, the design of the Center includes a beautiful floor to ceiling glass wall between the Children's Room and the area where clients interact with social workers, counselors, and other professionals. Alameda County designed a similar set up and many other Centers have followed suit but Mexico gets credit for an innovative design very early in this movement.

Today, the FJC movement in Mexico is alive and growing. President Felipe Calderon is looking closely at the model and developing plans for a number of pilot Centers across the country, working in close partnership with the Family Justice Center Alliance. It is a vital need in Mexico and their leadership can open the doors to Central and South America with their determination to bring services together in desperately needy communities where violence is far too acceptable and services are far too minimal. The Mexican government sees the vision—even if there are few services for a community, those few services will be far more effective working together than staying separated and isolated from each other.

Amman, Jordan

The opening of the first two Centers in Amman, Jordan has been one of the most gratifying areas of work for our team in many years. Our new online book on the experience in Jordan and the principles we have identified from our work in Jordan that can guide the creation of more Centers in the Middle East has been an exciting project.[2] The

Hashemite Kingdom of Jordan has been working on family protection issues for over a decade. They have passed a status law, passed a domestic violence law, created a multi-disciplinary model through the Family Protection Department, and helped shape the dialogue on issues of family violence throughout the Middle East.

This foundation of activism, specialization, and government leadership was critical to moving toward co-located services. One of my most vivid memories on one of my first trips to Jordan was meeting Dr. Manal Tahtamouni. She is an OB-GYN in Amman who is a visionary and pioneer in the concept of co-locating services for women who are victims of abuse. She leads a Women's Health Clinic sponsored by Queen Noor. During the queen's tenure, the clinic took seriously the need for health services for poor women in Amman. But Dr. Tahtamouni went further. She started asking her patients what other services they needed. She started assessing for family violence. She added coffee times, yoga classes, and social services. Her patients identified the issues of domestic violence and said they wished their husbands could get some help early on in their marriages. So, Dr. Tahtamouni started classes for new Muslim husbands at the clinic. She even made sure they stayed focus on the teachings of the Prophet Mohammed in the process. On the wall of the meeting room, in Arabic, she had her staff paint the words of the Prophet, "Above all, care for the women." How wise! How powerful was the vision and passion of one woman in a poor community in central Amman.

Vital Voices Global Partnership reached out to the Family Justice Center Alliance as Jordan began to look more closely at the Family Justice Center movement in the United States and we were able to garner powerful support from the U.S. Department of State. And relationships mattered. I bonded with the men. Gael bonded with the women. On one trip, Gael and prosecutor Tim Campen were able to meet with Queen Rania and share the dream, the benefits of co-location, and give her a copy of our first book on the FJC vision.

Over a period of two years, with the support of Shireen Zaman, Dana Al-Ebrahim, Cindy Dyer, and the entire team at Vital Voices Global Partnership we helped them build on their ten years of developing policies, protocols, and procedures that preceded our arrival. We engaged in strategic planning with one of our gifted planners, Judi Adams, with the support of the King and Queen, partnered with local experts, consultants, talked to survivors, and helped start two pilot Centers in Jordan. One, the Queen Rania Child and Family Center, is an expansion of an existing children's resource center. The other, Dar Al-Wefaq, is a domestic violence shelter sponsored by the Ministry of Social Development. But both models have evaluated the principles of co-located, multi-agency services and then applied them in a culturally appropriate way in their country.

Jordan set an excellent example for communities around the world by conducting focus groups with survivors before we completed the planning process. They also recruited two local consultants with a strong background in domestic violence advocacy—Samar Haj Hasan and Yasmine Pharoan—from Mahara Consulting Services. Samar and Yasmine did it right. They asked the following questions of all survivors:

Please provide detailed answers to the following questions in six different organizations or current points of entry for victims:[3]

- What are the factors or (situation, incidents) that has led you to visit this location?

- How did you hear about this program?

- If you were referred, who referred you?

- What are the services that were provided to you at this organization?

- What are the services that you wanted, but were not provided at or by this center?

- Were you referred to other organizations or institutions to provide you with the services that were lacking in this center?

- What are the challenges, if any (all sorts of challenges) you faced in obtaining services that were not provided by this place?

- What services would you like to see added to this center so we can provide comprehensive services for protecting and supporting victims of violence in one place?

- Are there any other services that you need but couldn't find anywhere? (at this place or any center or institution in Jordan)

- And finally, if we were able to offer all services for victims of violence under one roof, what's your idea and vision of this center, what would you imagine the center to look like? What services would you like to see in place to help and assist you and your family? And finally, how are the services being provided? Please provide us with an elaborate answer.

The focus groups provided powerful feedback that drove the planning process in Jordan and can provide direction to many other communities. The victims wanted all their services in one place. They wanted legal protection from their abusers. They wanted someone to clearly tell their husbands that the violence was wrong. They identified medical services, social services, counseling, recreation, and spiritual support as all critical to an effective Center. They did not want to leave their families or their husbands so they wanted the Center to help facilitate couples counseling and safe, monitored recreational trips for the whole family. But they wanted to know they could come back whenever necessary. They wanted to have secret interaction with the courts so that public shame did not come to them or their families. Their feedback was so rich when asked to design a Center and be "elaborate." They wanted drama therapy, vocational training that would allow them to make money while being at home with their children, visits to their home to check up on their well being regularly, and a hotline number to call the Center any time they needed to talk to someone.

Perhaps what struck us the most was that over and over they said they wanted to be—shown respect and treated with dignity. They wanted all partners to work together closely with a clear focus on working together to help them. They described agency staff at places that had ridiculed them, made fun of them, or laughed at them. They talked of being blamed, lectured, and berated.[4] They knew exactly what a great co-location model should look like and they wanted it! Half way around the world from the Family Justice Center movement in the United States, women in Amman, Jordan who had never been to a Family Justice Center conference, never been offered a federal grant, and never read any of our books, wanted a Family Justice Center!

On a recent trip, we toured both newly created co-location models. The art program at the Queen Rania Center grabbed my heart as we watched children drawing pictures and text from the International Declaration of Human Rights related to family violence! Then, later that day, near dark, we toured the Dar Al-Wefaq. The four story building is housing for women and children on the second, third, and fourth floors. The first floor has been configured for partner agencies to bring staff to provide multi-agency, multi-disciplinary services for victims and their children. They did well. There is a beautiful children's room, interview rooms, a medical exam room, counseling rooms, a training room, and a kitchen and dining room. But what grabbed me most happened as we left the building at the end of the tour. It was dark and we were walking out of the courtyard to our bus. As we walked away, I turned back for one last look. There in the windows on the second, third, and fourth floors I could see women and children looking out at us. Many were behind the drapes, most had their heads covered by a hijab. The children were holding on to or holding hands with their mothers. But there they were watching us. I paused, smiled, and then decided to wave. I wanted to express my care. I wanted them to know how proud I was of them. And they waved back. Suddenly, I saw smiles on faces, wild waving, and children laughing at the crazy American. I started to cry. What amazing heroic women. In a culture with few options, facing shaming from their families and their abusers families, they were standing up for their rights. They were in a concrete block building surrounded by a rock wall with barbwire on the top making a statement about their worth and their value. They were the founders of the first Family Justice Center in Jordan. One day, may their courage, lead the way for thousands of others across the Middle East to pursue our vision. Enshala…

DOES EVERY COUNTRY AND EVERY COMMUNITY HAVE TO FOLLOW THE JOURNEY OF THE WESTERN BATTERED WOMEN'S MOVEMENT?

In November 2009, the trip to Jordan for the opening of the Centers involved hosting the first ever regional conference in the Middle East on Family Justice Centers. We had teams from 12 countries under the sponsorship of the Middle East Partnership Initiative.[5] It is always challenging to work in a country where you don't speak the language and the Middle East is high on that list. We had over one hundred participants, men and women, from across the region and the whole conference was translated into Arabic for the participants. Working through translators is always entertaining. You tell a joke and no one laughs. You say something very serious and smiles erupt around the room. You talk for a thirty seconds and your translator says one word in Arabic! You think you said, "It is such an honor to be here. You all have the power to change the world for victims of family violence and their children." But it is very possible that the translator just said, "I am related to baboons and my mother should never have let me out of the house when I was a child. You are all smart to run when I suggest anything."

Nevertheless, it was an historic event and it will shape the future in the Middle East.

But some key questions arose during our time working in the Middle East. One of the most significant was the title of this section. Does every country and every community have to follow the journey of the western battered women's movement? The others that came up were just as significant. Does child abuse have to be a focus before violence against women? Do we have to do shelters before we do coordinated community response? Does everyone have to silo in their agencies and disciplines before we look at how to work together or even how to co-locate?

These questions will not all be answered in the brief pages of this book! But they are worth much thought. As we met with them, it was clear that status laws that give legal status to women are a crucial foundation for much of our work in family violence intervention and prevention. Such laws were crucial in the west and they will likely be crucial in the Middle East and other parts of the world. A society ordains what it will and won't tolerate by its laws. The rule of law is central to the enforcement of human rights in many arenas.[6] But many of the other questions might be answered in the negative, or perhaps with more questions. Why do we have to wait to collaborate around the world until everyone is not collaborating? Why does a focus on child abuse have to come before we deal with violence against women? We know that you cannot protect children if you do not protect their mothers. So, why not start with protecting their mothers? We need shelters for those in the most danger in every part of the world. But in cultures where there is so little support or social assistance after going into a shelter, why not spend more time developing prevention initiatives?[7] If the stigma is so powerful around reporting or systems intervention, why not start with the health clinic model?

In the Middle East and many other places around the world, it is safe for women to get health services. Even in the most male dominated societies on earth, they want their women to be healthy. So, let's think strategically about this. We would never have done this in the United States but it could be powerful in other parts of the world.

Such thinking also illustrates another key piece of sending the concepts of coordination, collaboration, and co-location around the world. Together, any group of people is more powerful than when they are apart. Social change is all about critical mass.[8] And critical mass is all about community organizing, coming together, and staying together around a common vision and purpose. President Obama taught us that as a community organizer and in his run for the White House. We have seen it in the Family Justice Center movement. When we bring teams to our conferences and send them home, they are more likely to get things done. When we have a large group working on creating a Center, it is much more likely to be successful. There is strength and power in numbers.

So, if the breast cancer awareness movement is powerful and accepted in countries around the world, we should be partnering with them on other critical services for women and children including services around sexual assault and domestic violence. If job training and economic empowerment has an open door, we should be looking to have services connected to family violence in such locations.

CONCLUSION

The whole world needs co-located services. The whole world needs collaborative, coordinated, networked groups of people working to stop violence and sexual assault against women and children. The whole world needs to connect women's health, women's rights, women's empowerment, women's legal protection, women's status, and women's economic opportunities with the violence and abuse that continues to permeate cultures from east to west. And survivors, advocates, and change agents (both men and women) in so many other countries have much to offer us in the United States. Their vision inspires us often. Their creativity often puts us to shame. The amount of advocacy, coordination, and protection that they provide with very few resources often puts us to shame. They need us. We need them. We are more powerful together. They are more powerful together. Spread the word!

NOTES

1 To get more information about the Centre, go to: http://www.saartjiebaart-mancentre.org.za/

2 See www.familyjusticecenter.org to download a copy of the new manual, in Arabic or English. The manual is entitled: "Hope for Hurting Families: A Guide to Co-Located Services in the Middle East."

3 The focus group questions were asked at the following agencies that partnered together: Jordan River Foundation—Queen Rania Family and Child Center; Noor Hussein Foundation—Institute for Family Health; Ministry of Justice—Human Rights and Family Affairs Department; Al Hussein Society for Habilitation/Rehabilitation of the Physically Challenged; Family and Child Protection Services; Family Protection Unit; and the National Center for Human Rights.

4 The Summary of the Jordanian focus groups are available upon request from the National Family Justice Center Alliance.

5 The Middle East Partnership Initiative is sponsored by the U.S. Department of State and has opened many doors in the Arab world to collaborations between east and west. It has also played a vital role in promoting initiatives that improve the status of women and promote public-private partnership efforts in the Middle East. For more information, go to: www.mepi.state.gov.

6 Rule of law is a general legal maxim according to which decisions should be made by applying known principles or laws, without the intervention of discretion in their application. The American Bar Association and many other organizations have been focused on advocating for laws on violence against women in the Middle East and Eastern Europe for many years and, without question, legal status for women and legal protections are critical to all that we might do in the Family Justice Center movement in the years to come.

7 At the time of this writing, the International Violence Against Women Act has been introduced in the U.S. Congress. Thanks to the leadership of the Esta Soler and the Family Violence Prevention Fund there is a strong international push toward prevention of violence against women around the world. The *International Violence Against Women Act* (*I-VAWA*) is the first comprehensive piece of legislation in the United States aimed at ending violence against women and girls around the world. The *I-VAWA* (HR 4594/S 2982) would improve our government's response when women and girls are victims of sex trafficking and rape during war and would provide aid to women's groups on the ground working to help survivors of domestic and sexual violence. It would focus resources on prevention and ensure that our dollars are used in the most effective ways possible to help the people who need it most. To view the legislation in its proposed form, go to: http://www.state.gov/r/pa/prs/ps/2010/02/136508.htm

8   See Malcom Gladwell, *The Tipping Point,* (2002) Back Bay Publishing. Many
     other excellent pieces have been written but Gladwell did an excellent job of
     explaining critical mass in social change theory and applying it to real life issues
     in the United States and around the world.

CHAPTER TEN

Reflections of a Dreamer

Gloria grew up in a residential neighborhood in the San Francisco Bay Area. She was involved in the Girl Scouts, Candy Stripers, and volunteered at a local mental hospital helping children. When she was 16 she started dating a boy who lived across the street. Despite his rough exterior, Gloria felt that he had a very soft heart and great potential. In retrospect, she thinks that the "fast" life intrigued her, and the fact that her parents didn't care for him appealed to a rebellious streak in her. But underneath it all her desire to help others made her think that she could change him. The verbal and emotional abuse began early in the relationship. In hindsight Gloria says she should have known, but there was little recognition or understanding of relationship abuse or domestic violence in the 1960s. People mostly assumed that if abuse happened, the person who was abused somehow deserved it.

Gloria intended for her first attempt to escape from her abuser to be her last. While she was studying for finals at the University of California at Berkeley, her boyfriend tried to get her to stop studying and spend time with him. When she insisted on studying, he screamed at her and accused her of being with other men. Gloria was so distraught and depressed that she threw herself out of a third-story window with the intent of killing herself. She survived but sustained a broken back. Gloria soon determined that nothing was going to stop her from getting her degree. She took her finals in a body cast, graduating from Berkeley with a B.A. in Sociology in only three years.

Despite the abuse, Gloria agreed to marry the boyfriend, but as Gloria became more accomplished professionally, the abuse increased and became more public. While she was working at the Alameda County Project Intercept, a job-training project for men and women convicted of first-time misdemeanors, her husband harassed her frequently with abusive phone calls and actually stormed into the office accusing her of sexual relations with her boss.

At 25 she had her first and only child. By then the physical abuse was severe. Early on, he had been careful not to hit her where bruises would show, but as time went by he didn't care about the blackened eyes or who would see them. People would tell him to stop, but he didn't. Gloria's father, one of the mainstays of her support system frequently would visit her to try to persuade her to go to the police, but she did not.

When Gloria became Executive Director of the Rape Crisis Center of Contra Costa County and Marin County, the violence got worse. He pulled a gun on her and threatened to kill her if she left—"If you go to the end of the earth, I'll find you," he said. As the head of a rape crisis center, she spoke daily to women about the right to be free of abuse in their lives, and then she would go home to unspeakable abuse herself.

She sought help from a priest. He told her to go home and be a good wife. It was devastating to be personally at risk and in a failing marriage and hear that if she left her husband, the church might excommunicate her. Would God would abandon her?

Despite his threats to kill her, Gloria tried to leave 10 times, but always came back. Finally she called the police for help. He ran off before the police arrived. She gives much credit to that officer for helping her make the decision to finally leave. He was knowledgeable about domestic violence and sensitive to her situation, a rare combination at that time. She remembers him saying to her, "You're the only one who can make your child's life different." And she remembers her 5-year-old son saying, "If you only did what Daddy told you to do, this wouldn't have happened!" Right then and there she told herself, "If I don't get out, this little boy is going to become that man." She sat on her bed in her room alone and wept feeling like a failure and not knowing what to do. Amidst the tears she felt a consoling voice say, "It's all right, Gloria. You did all you could do." The priest was wrong, God had not abandoned her.

So she gathered up her son and a few things and left to live in a motel in a secret location for two months. She finally was able to return to the house, but she had to change the locks to keep her husband from walking in at any time unannounced. She endured months of ongoing stalking, harassment, and more abuse before she was finally free. She regularly called a local domestic violence organization (now called STAND!) for advice and safety planning. The calls she made were anonymous because as executive director of a local rape crisis center she felt she could not expose herself and risk revealing the incredible conflict between her professional and personal lives.

Today, Gloria Sandoval is the Executive Director of the very agency she called for advice as a victim. She manages a $6 million annual budget and oversees a staff of over 100. She has been recognized locally and statewide with awards and accolades. She advocated for the creation of a Zero Tolerance to Domestic Violence Policy in Contra Costa County. She is using her experience, leadership gifts, and power to help advocate for the creation of the West Contra Costa County Family Justice Center. Gloria is still a dreamer. She keeps dreaming big dreams and challenges everyone around her to remember that we are not done yet. We have much more to do and we cannot simply try to maintain or preserve what we have. Gloria says it best, "We must keep reaching, we must keep advocating, we must keep learning. There is no other way to change the world."

Gloria Sandoval is one of my heroes. She is a dreamer. She is a doer. She is relentless. She is unstoppable. Always moving forward, always humble, and always encouraging others to dream with her. She is a great example for all of us who have any part in the massive effort that we call the domestic violence movement. The movement should follow Gloria's example—keep moving, stay humble as we go, and keep encouraging and supporting each other as we dream big and never stop dreaming. Let's share some reflections on moving forward, encouraging each other, and dreaming or supporting our dreamers before we finish the "why" book on the exciting, new, rapidly developing Family Justice Center movement.

WE ALL NEED TO MAKE SURE WE KEEP MOVING FORWARD

Many, besides Gloria Sandoval, are talking about the need for the domestic violence movement to keep evolving and co-located services are part of this future. One recent study by Dr. Nicole Allen and Dr. Amy Lehrner has helped frame some of the issues that we should all be thinking about as we move forward.

Dr. Lehrner and Dr. Allen developed an excellent small scale study that focused on assessing the movement through in-depth interviews with advocates working for domestic violence policy and direct service organizations. Their analysis then focused on three critical issues: 1) advocates' reflections on the state of the domestic violence movement; 2) challenges and dilemmas facing the movement; and 3) advocates' visions for the future.[1]

Their primary conclusions and observations form the foundation for a powerful dialogue in the months and years to come. First, they found that few of the advocates working in the trenches knew the history of the movement. "With no foundation in the history of the movement or its analysis, participants framed the work and goals of domestic violence agencies in terms of service provision", they wrote, with little understanding of the socio-political context of domestic violence. Though public awareness and outreach were a priority for some, there was little context for such priorities. They also found that advocates lacked the guiding, overarching, principles that should be the foundation for such priorities and which provide an understanding of the causes of domestic violence.

Second, the researchers found that because of the journey of the movement, and the resources and allies that have joined the movement over the last thirty years, there has been a waning of the social change orientation of the movement toward a "professionalization" and "therapeutically oriented social service agenda." Such a phenomenon is natural in social changes movements but not necessarily a positive step.

Third, most women of color who participated in the study viewed the movement as a "white women's movement" and described a strong sense that the movement as a whole has failed to understand cultural context and alienated many who do not see violence only through explicitly feminist gender politics. This blind spot has often ignored the significance and impact of discrimination and racism in looking at the impacts of violence and abuse in the lives of women of color.

Finally, they pointed out how little mentoring is going on in a movement that needs to produce the next generation of innovators, leaders, and change agents. Many advocates who were interviewed complained about the lack of mentoring and coaching from those who came before them. Indeed, the administrators who were interviewed were not holders of the history and therefore had little ability to pass it on to others.

Lehrner and Allen describe much of what they heard in this way: "...safety for victims might require hiding them but...advocates who consider this the extent of their work do so at their peril. In addition to protecting victim safety, movement advocates must cultivate collaborations and openness with local communities. Historically, this has proven difficult when the values and politics of movement advocates and community members were not necessarily in alignment." The advocates in the study who saw this issue pointed out that "failure to engage with local communities constrains both the nature of interventions with victims and the possibilities for creative new approaches to social change." The authors conclude that these dynamics and the inability of the movement founders and leading feminist shelter organizations to focus on much more than crisis intervention and survival has had a powerful devolutionary effect. "The end result is a potential devolution of the movement into the exclusive provision of direct services concurrent with a shifting service philosophy that conceptualizes intervention as the provision of mental health services." Such a result will not lead to empowerment of survivors of domestic violence or to a victim-centered, victim autonomy focus.

In fairness to many in the movement who have been reaching out to build partnerships and collaborations for decades; the study fails to really acknowledge just how many successful efforts have been made locally, nationally, and internationally to build partnerships and collaborations. It also fails to really examine the powerful barriers and hostility that the movement has run into at so many points from entrenched interests, anti-feminist value systems, sexist value systems, and male-dominated civil and criminal justice systems.

It fascinates me that the ideas raised in the study were all identified by advocates in community-based domestic violence organizations. It was not made up by those in the criminal or civil justice systems, the child welfare community, the medical profession, the faith community, or others who came late to the journey. The call to mentor those who come behind us, the reminder to stay committed to the social change and advocacy focus of the movement, the need to think outside the box, and the call to honor our history but be willing to continue to pursue innovation, collaboration, and community mobilization and engagement strategies (no matter what the obstacles or opposition), *came from those who are officially "inside" the historical core of the movement.* Now, all of us who care about stopping domestic violence and promoting the ongoing "movement" need to take heed and…move… forward. We are not done. We have not found all the ways yet to stop intimate partner violence. The vast majority of those in our communities and in our country are still not engaged in our dreams and passions for this work. The volume of the message is still muted in the everyday lives of most Americans. Has progress been made? Yes. Should we celebrate the successes of the last 20 years? Yes. But too many people still need to join us.

Their study should cause all of us who care about violence in the family to think through what it says even if we don't agree with it and even if they did not do justice to the amazing, successful, powerful collaborative efforts that have occurred. How do we continue to cherish and honor our feminist roots and the importance of the gender analysis critical to understanding most domestic violence while also acknowledging the powerful ways we must keep moving forward?

How do we address violence in gay and lesbian relationships, violence by women, and the complex dynamics of generational abuse perceived as normative by young people? How do we keep innovating, trying new approaches to social change, community mobilization, co-location of services, the development of local communities of diverse advocates who then help change the local culture and values around the issue of domestic violence? How do we avoid fighting over the small pie we all split instead of working together to make the pie so very much bigger? How do we avoid the trend toward treating all domestic violence victims as prospective mental health clients?

I am hopeful. The work of Ellen Pence and the Advocacy Institute that OVW is funding is an excellent step forward. The work of Esta Soler and the Family Violence Prevention Fund in the national and international prevention arena should cause us all to think more proactively. The work of Denise Gamache and the Battered Women's Justice Project to make sure our training is state of the art of always evidence-based is a critical component of relevance and credibility. The outreach and training of Agnes Maldonado and Alianza to and for state domestic violence coalitions nationwide has moved forward the commitment to diversity in the movement. The vision and thinking of Dr. Oliver Williams at the Institute for Domestic Violence in the African American Community has opened the dialogue on many subjects not often talked about that impact African-American women and men. The leadership of Gael Strack at the National Family Justice Center Alliance has challenged all of us to be more engaged in bringing agencies and disciplines together while seeking to stay true to guiding principles from the core of the movement. The leadership of Sue Else and her growing strategic partnerships with business and corporate leaders and her challenge to local, state, and national programs to keep evolving, looking outward, and growing --- are all very positive steps forward. But there is still too much tension whenever we talk about new ideas or innovative approaches in local communities. Often those who want to do both social change and service delivery together, get charged with ignoring "victim safety" or "confidentiality" the hallmark words at the core of the movement. But we must ultimately have many more solutions to the social problem of family violence.

The domestic violence movement must reach out more proactively to the child welfare movement. The Greenbook Initiative made clear how important it is for the domestic violence movement to continue the many ways that the domestic violence movement has reached out over the years. But we must keep reaching out and framing the issues around children exposed from a domestic violence perspective. We must be more creative in creating services for male victims of domestic violence and we must be more diligent in applying what we have learned about wraparound services for victims to the massive need to provide wraparound services for aggressors. We cannot stop. We cannot slow down because we are tired. We cannot rest because there are so many barriers to efforts at relationship building and partnerships. We cannot become hardened to the ongoing call for change from those within the movement itself simply because we are cynical of the young, the energetic, and the creative.

The leadership of the Blue Shield of California Foundation has rightly challenged us in California to focus on the critical importance of leadership in the movement and in our organizations, on mentoring of the next generation, and on succession planning. They have also challenged us to critically analyze our organizations, our structures, and our strategic directions as we move forward. Other powerful foundations like Robert Wood Johnson, Allstate, Verizon, Avon, and others are all looking for the movement to keep moving, growing, evolving, changing, and advancing. They don't want to simply pass out small dollars for minimal impact. They want major impacts and major progress as they invest their dollars. They want us to help them to change the world. It is a blessing to have strong leaders in the corporate philanthropic world who understand the crucial importance of the movement to keep moving...forward. The economic landscape is strewn with businesses that did not keep adapting, changing, and evolving. Major brand names that were thriving ten years ago are now gone or barely surviving. Why? Because they did not adapt, did not listen enough to their customers, and did not keep forming strategic alliances. It is a powerful reminder to keep listening to survivors as we move forward.

Recently, in Richmond, California we heard from a courageous survivor during a planning meeting for the West Contra Costa County Family Justice Center. "Rhonda" stood before us and said these words: "Please don't forget how hard it is for us to get out and get help. Please keep listening, please keep figuring out how to help in better ways, and please include us as you go forward."

As noted earlier in the book, Mary Claire Landry in New Orleans heard many voices like Rhonda's after Hurricane Katrina. She rallied her friends and colleagues and challenged everyone to dream big with a total focus on the needs of survivors. The result became the creation of the New Orleans Family Justice Center, a shelter-led co-located services model with key support from the U.S. Department of Justice, the City of New Orleans, local nonprofit agencies, and the community. Mary Claire has become a vital and powerful voice in the national domestic violence movement because of her passion and her vision.

WE ALL NEED TO BE ENCOURAGERS, TO BE AFFIRMERS

Recently, my daughters and my son, all independent of each other, told me how much they loved me and shared with me how much the affirmation and encouragement of our home had meant to them. Kelly called me, Karianne sent me a Facebook message, and Chris told me how much he appreciated me and then wrapped his arms around me! It made me cry. They were giving me what my wife Beth and I have tried to give them their whole lives. We have tried to be their biggest cheerleaders. We have tried to be the supporters of their dreams. We have tried to often remind them that they have divine callings in life and God-given gifts and abilities to use to help others and make a difference in the world. Now, as they become adults they are gifting us with the very encouragement we have tried to instill in their lives for over 20 years. Does it get any better than that? Encouragement changes the world.

The grace of God and the mercy of my children certainly play

While Hurricane Katrina was devastating to New Orleans, I also saw it as an incredible opportunity. Every single system was destroyed—Crescent House Shelter burned to the ground, the Police Department, the District Attorney's office, the courthouses, all were flooded. Every single agency in the city lost their ability to operate and every single person in the city was in survival mode. If in a moment's notice, your world, as you know it was destroyed, and rebuilding was the order of the day, the question to be asked is "If I had a blank slate, would my services look the same?" Katrina provided that blank slate—despite all the tragedy, the pain and the trauma—and gave us the opportunity to re-think, re-vision and to listen to the voices of survivors. Every aspect of our services was re-designed based on the needs of survivors. We were challenged to think differently about housing and service delivery. Within months of the disaster it made sense to offer our trailer at Crescent House to the domestic violence unit of the NOPD—the partnership was vital to our very survival. It was the beginning of co-location. With neighborhoods and systems destroyed, co-locating services in one place was the only model that made sense. We joined forces with our criminal justice and civil legal partners and our survivors to create the vision of the center. Against great odds, the collaboration was forged, immovable systems began to change, turf battles were minimized, and effective client centered services continue to emerge. It is truly a testament to the passion, determination and a resilience of the people of our community. We simply won't give up.

Mary Claire Landry, Director
Crescent House (Catholic Charities)
New Orleans Family Justice Center

a role in all of this. I was not the perfect father or parent. I was too many times impatient, too many times self-absorbed, and so many times too busy to really just sit and listen to them without distraction. I was at times more critical of them and their friends than I needed to be. But perhaps love does cover a multitude of sins and the conscious choice to always err on the side of affirmation and encouragement was never a mistake. A long time ago, my Dad told me that I could never be too supportive of my kids, too positive about their abilities, or too encouraging of them to pursue their dreams. He was right. You can never be too positive. You can easily be too critical, too judgmental, and too angry but you can never be too positive. The note below reminds of the power of affirmation and the importance of

Karen, thanks again for your help today. As always, you went above and beyond for a very vulnerable victim and your assistance is greatly appreciated. I know that you had a very busy day but you still allowed me to page you if I needed assistance (which I did) and you were able to connect with the victim and set her up with counseling. That is why we do what we do and this is what it is all about. The High Risk Review Team will be considering the defendant on the High Risk Offender list. Pam, when you said it is all about relationships, you were so right. (I never doubted you!). Even though I am no longer at the Center every day, I still know where to call, as I know, I cannot do my job without the likes of the Partners at the FVP.

Note from a Prosecutor to an Advocate and FJC Director
Mosaic Counseling and Family Services (Ontario, Canada)

professionals sharing their successes with each other. It was sent from a prosecutor to an advocate and to "Pam", the Center's Director.

A number of years ago, two psychologists named Gary Smalley and John Trent wrote a book called "The Blessing" and focused on the power of a parent's blessing being given to a child. They looked back thousands of years in Jewish history and examined what the elements of that blessing are when done properly. Here it is: A FAMILY BLESSING BEGINS WITH MEANINGFUL TOUCHING. IT CONTINUES WITH A SPOKEN MESSAGE OF HIGH VALUE, A MESSAGE THAT PICTURES A SPECIAL FUTURE FOR THE INDIVIDUAL BEING BLESSED, AND ONE THAT IS BASED ON AN ACTIVE COMMITMENT TO SEE THE BLESSING COME TO PASS. Giving the blessing to others changes the world.

My wife and I tried very imperfectly to deliver that blessing to each of our children as they grew up in our home. And as I reflected on how it has come full circle now it caused me to start reflecting on the power of words and actions of blessing, affirmation, and encouragement in the rest of my life. Children thrive with it, and shrivel without it. Friends shine brighter with words and actions of support and they often feel unappreciated it and even hurt when we withhold those words. Co-workers feel validated and noticed when we offer such spirit-lifting lifeblood and feel ignored and disrespected when we don't give offer them. The Bible says that words of encouragement are words that give grace to those who hear them. I try hard to be an encourager around the San Diego FJC, at the FJC Alliance, and with many that I fellowship with around the country. It doesn't mean I have not had to confront poor leadership or improper actions at times. But it does mean I don't want the negative to define me. I really want the positive to be my legacy. And when I am the recipient of positive notes, cards, emails, and spoken words of edification, encouragement, and support…I feel stronger, more inspired to keep going, and more energized to stand strong in the face of opposition. When I don't give enough of it, I often miss opportunities to celebrate excellence, giftedness, and acts of service given to those in need by others around me.

While working a while ago with Melissa Mack, our Director of Technical Assistance, at the Tulsa Family Safety Center (one of our nearly 60 Family Justice Centers currently operating in the United States), I saw the power of encouragement in a Center first hand. I heard the courageous stories of their clients in a focus group we hosted and was able to tell each of them how much I admired them and how proud I was to see their heroic stories of survival. One woman said, "I am not just a survivor, I am an overcomer." Another said, "The abuse has not destroyed me, it has helped me become the strong woman I am today." I loved giving them words of appreciation and encouragement. They spoke words of encouragement to us and we to them. We did not ignore the challenges or the struggles but we found ways to express appreciation to them for determination, passion, commitment, a refusal to shrink back, and a community commitment to move forward and be even better at meeting the needs of victims and their children.

There were a few negative folks in some of the meetings. It was amazing how one negative person could suck so much energy from others. One person without the ability to see the good and the positive amidst the challenges was able to discourage others. But clearly Tulsa has focused more on the positive than the negative. They have chosen affirmation instead of criticism. They have chosen a positive "We can do it" attitude instead of a negative "We can't do that" attitude. They are a great example to other communities and a great challenge to all of us personally. So, as we come to the conclusion of this book and you think about your work in a Center, your support for a local Center, or your opportunity to be part of starting a Center, let me challenge you.

Are you an encourager? Or are you a discourager? Do others feel supported in your presence? Or do they feel simply anger, disappointment, and judgment? Do you try to find the best in others or do you suffer from a critical spirit? Maybe you are burned out or cynicism has spread in your life like a cancer. Maybe you have gotten too self absorbed to really care about the pain of others. Maybe you are too focused on what your job is and not enough on what it means to love and care for others. Domestic violence victims need even more encouragement than many of us who have not been abused. They have been ordered around, manipulated, and put down. They have been told so often no one else wants them, that they are stupid, that they do nothing right. So many children in a violent home have been told they will never amount to anything, that they were a mistake, or that they are part of the problem. Then they end up in our agencies and in our Family Justice Centers. And we might be tempted to move toward case plans, rules, classes, system responses, and coordinating what needs to happen instead of taking the time to play a game, read them a book, offer them food and a chance to just talk. Maybe they need someone to first tell them how proud we are that they are supporting their mom, how courageous they have been to get through what they have seen and experienced.

Many Centers now do monthly client appreciation lunches and parties like we have learned from Croydon, England. In San Diego, we celebrate our amazing women through our VOICES Committee where we honor them, celebrate them, praise them, and elevate them. VOICES is a group of former FJC clients that are referred to the group by a counselor at the Center, Dr. Diane Lass, when it is clear they are ready to speak about their experience. They become advocates, public proponents, and community educators. They speak at City Council meetings and regularly conduct media interviews to educate everyone about the benefits they received through co-located services and why others should support the vision and the work. They are an amazing group of women and powerful allies if you want to develop and preserve and evolve a victim-centered service model. They review our new projects and ideas. They help critique new products being offered to clients at the San Diego FJC. Other Centers are now following San Diego's lead in developing their own versions of a VOICES Committee.

In many Centers and community-based agencies, children get gifts and presents to communicate love, appreciation, acceptance, and encouragement. Many Family Justice Centers and other co-located service models are following this example. We should be gift givers and communicators and never forget the encouragement and affirmation are some of the greatest gifts of all. Let's follow my Dad's advice to me many times in life before he died: "You can never be too encouraging or too positive." Researchers have already figured it out. Encouragement creates resiliency in children. One person who passionately believes in a woman or a child that has been abused can do more than twenty programs or fifteen referrals. I remember one woman who told me that the advocate that hugged her every day she came in became the arms of God wrapping around her every time she showed up at the FJC. God often needs our arms, our words, our smiles, and our warmth in order to communicate with those in terrible pain and mourning such profound loss and struggle.

Today, smile at a client you see, offer a piece of candy to a child, ask a couple questions and tell a little boy or a little girl how happy you are to have them there. Don't just leave it to someone else to do. As Gandhi said, be the change you want to see in the world. Be the encourager. Be the one who speaks life, hope, affirmation, and encouragement. You might be surprised how much your humble, loving, and thoughtful words and acts of kindness can change the world for those around you.

WE ALL NEED TO DREAM BIG OR MAKE SURE WE SUPPORT DREAMERS

Big visions and big dreams are great but getting them to reality is often difficult. I often joke when I speak at conferences around the world that dreaming and vision casting is tough work. I remind folks that there is only one difference between a vision and a hallucination—the number of people who see it! So, if you have a vision for your community and no one else sees it, you need counseling and medication! But if you have a dream and other people can see it and you can join your lives together to pursue it, you can help make that dream a reality. And I love seeing communities that have figured it out.

One of the newest Family Justice Centers is in Montgomery, Alabama. They are a living testimony to communities across the United States and around the world. They have been dreaming big about the first Family Justice Center in Alabama for nearly ten years. This very dedicated group of government and community leaders was disappointed to learn after years of advocating that they did not receive a federal grant they had been seeking to fund the opening of a Center. It was the second time they had applied for a federal FJC grant and had not been funded. In the midst of a very bad economy, they were deeply discouraged. They had asked me to come and celebrate their announcement of a grant or perhaps even a Grand Opening and now they called to say there was no need for me to come. They were calling to let me know they did not get their grant. But as we talked on the phone it was clear to me their dream was still strong. They were determined and unwilling to give up. So, I agreed to donate my time and come anyway and rally the community and they agreed to keep advocating. I told them we should re-double our vision casting, outreach, press push, and elevate our voices to recruit caring public officials and business leaders. And they did!

Less than a month after being notified of their grant denial, we had a breakfast for the community, tours of their agencies, a luncheon with local elected officials, and a press conference with the Chief Justice of their Supreme Court, Sue Bell Cobb (just blocks from the church of Dr. Martin Luther King Jr.). The District Attorney, Ellen Brooks, was clearly the leader. She was passionate, determined, and focused. Her Assistant DA, Daryl Bailey, was equally committed. I met Karen Sellers, who runs the local shelter. What a zealous advocate! She chose not to see the FJC as a threat but as a step forward. I met a dedicated police Lt. named Steve Searcy from the Montgomery Police Department and many others. The Montgomery Advertiser newspaper endorsed their cause. Faith and business community leaders joined the coalition that day. And I began to see why Montgomery is such a special place. In the middle of a terrible economy, without a federal grant, with government facing major cuts, I learned that the Mayor of Montgomery, Todd Strange, "got it", and realized that the FJC was a life and death issue for everyone. I met Donnie Mims, the County Administrator, and a man of great integrity, who attended our events for most of the day and listened thoughtfully to all the issues. Many local survivors stepped up to be counted, share their stories, and support the vision. And by the end of the day, without a federal grant, and without any formal commitment of funds by anyone, the dream was alive and dynamic because of the amazing people of Montgomery, Alabama.

What a lesson for my own community and so many others across the United States and around the world. They did not get a federal grant. They are in a terrible economy. They are cutting budgets and facing tough decisions every day about priorities. But they did not abandon their dream for a Family Justice Center. In fact, they advocated all the more aggressively. They created a plan to buy a building. They asked the County and the City to work together to make it all happen. They committed full-time, on-site personnel from the Police Department, the District Attorney's Office, the shelter, and many other service providers. And they kept advocating...setting aside egos, turf issues, political calculations...just people joining their lives together to change the world for victims and their children and not take "No" for an answer. And they got it done!

Weeks after they refused to let the dream die, the Montgomery Advertiser announced that the Mayor had committed $300,000 from the City and the County had committed $300,000 to match it. Today, the dream of the Montgomery County Family Justice Center is a reality. They are now part of the "unstoppables"—those communities that will not be stopped in creating a powerful a Family Justice Center to save families. They are an example for everyone who shares the vision of all agencies working together in a community and is willing to make supporting the FJC a top priority. And did I tell you? The economy is really bad and Montgomery, Alabama did not get a federal grant.

CONCLUSION

The Family Justice Center movement is about dreaming big. It is a simple idea that is very complicated in its implementation. Ask survivors if they want to come one place for the services they need or go many places. Ask them what services they want there. And then do it. Bring staff members from many agencies to one place. Organize with victim safety and victim autonomy in mind. Create processes to help everyone come together and stay together as they all do their work with many of the same families. Keep asking clients how you are doing and then make changes based on their input. Stay humble, stay positive, encourage each other, support each other, keep dreaming while you do the work. Change the world.

NOTES

1   To view a power point overview of the article by Nicole Allen and Amy
    Lehrner, click on: http://www.blueshieldcafoundation.org/assets/files/reports/
    Tensions%20and%20Opportunities%20in%20the%20Domestic%20Vio-
    lence%20Movement.pdf

Breinigsville, PA USA
15 August 2010
243629BV00004B/2/P